Unknown Warrior

Unknown Warrior

The search for Australia's greatest Ace

Mike Rosel

Pen & Sword
AVIATION

The author and the publisher have sought to contact the copyright holders of works referred to in this text. In some instances it was not possible to do so, and any query in this regard should be directed to the original publisher.

First published in Australia in 2012 by Australian Scholarly Publishing Pty Ltd,
7 Lt Lothian St Nth, North Melbourne, Vic 3051
and reprinted in this format in 2014 by
Pen and Sword Aviation

An imprint of
Pen & Sword Books Ltd
47 Church Street
Barnsley
South Yorkshire
S70 2AS

ISBN 978 1 78346 394 7

Typeset by
Ophelia Leviny for Australian Scholarly Publishing Pty Ltd.
and by Mac Style Ltd, Bridlington, East Yorkshire for Pen and Sword Books Ltd.

Printed and bound in England
By CPI Group (UK) Ltd, Croydon, CR0 4YY

Pen & Sword Books Ltd incorporates the imprints of Pen & Sword Archaeology, Atlas, Aviation, Battleground, Discovery, Family History, History, Maritime, Military, Naval, Politics, Railways, Select, Transport, True Crime, and Fiction, Frontline Books, Leo Cooper, Praetorian Press, Seaforth Publishing and Wharncliffe.

For a complete list of Pen & Sword titles please contact
PEN & SWORD BOOKS LIMITED
47 Church Street, Barnsley, South Yorkshire, S70 2AS, England
E-mail: enquiries@pen-and-sword.co.uk
Website: www.pen-and-sword.co.uk

Contents

Dedication

To my supportive and very patient wife Maureen, who now knows more of the first air war than she considers necessary, and to our children and grandchildren, who may appreciate here individual and collective loss beyond understanding on both sides of wars.

And to my late father, VX48603 Lt John Rosel, who would never talk to his six children of what a former Melbourne bank clerk endured in 1941 to win a Military Cross as one of the Rats of Tobruk. His children agreed with the English poet Chaucer, writing of another warrior almost 600 years earlier: 'A verray parfit gentil knyghte'.

Prologue

The ticking sound of a cooling aero engine dies away. The last blood drips. The peace of a spring night returns to the crash site in northern France where a young Australian pilot lies in his crushed fighter.

The smaller hunters of the night, briefly stilled by the sound of wood splintering and wires snapping, resume their search for prey in the woods and rolling farmland outside the small village of Noeux in the Pas de Calais region.

By 5am next morning—28 May 1918—a gendarme had carried news of the dead aviator to Major Charles Booker, commanding 201 Squadron in the newly-created Royal Air Force.

Booker approached the 'completely wrecked' Sopwith Camel and was shocked to find that he knew the dead pilot well—he had flown beside him above the Western Front.

Booker had to inform 203 Squadron pilots that their acting squadron commander, Captain Robert Alexander Little, had died in combat. The remarkable and protracted luck of Australia's most successful fighter pilot had finally run out during his solo night search for a Gotha bomber. The much-decorated Little was officially credited with a tally of 47 aerial victories, making him the most successful Australian Ace of all wars. In the Great War, he ranked eighth of all British Commonwealth Aces and fourteenth of all Aces from both sides.

Against all the odds, he had survived primitive flying training, a score or more of forced landings, fragile aircraft, a threat to withdraw his commission in the Royal Naval Air Service, and air combat over three years. He did not reach the last summer of the

Great War that would claim more than eight million soldiers' lives and perhaps five million civilians.

Among his peers, he was famous; the British awarded him the Distinguished Service Order (DSO) and Bar and the Distinguished Service Cross (DSC) and Bar, and France added the Croix de Guerre. His deadly shooting and aggressiveness had earned him the squadron nickname 'Rikki', after the mongoose which kills two cobras in one of Rudyard Kipling's hugely popular children's tales from *The Jungle Book*.

While *The Times* of London paid succinct tribute, Alec Little's home town papers in Melbourne, briefed by his proud father, eulogised his valour in the patriotic extremes of the time. *The Herald* outdid them all in an obituary headed *Death and Glory: Noted Australian Airman Meets The Fate Of A Hero*, with his photograph captioned *In Honor's Cause*. After outlining Little's remarkable career, the journalist presumed 'a sense of loss by every Australian who admires heroism and daring' and concluded 'Australia will remember the young airman who came forward unafraid in the hour of peril, scorning, as he said himself, to live the life of "an old coward"... before he perished he wrote his name in the sky, and he died on the wings of fame.'

In the annals of Scotch College, his old school, the legend recalled him as having flown with streamers in school colours on his wingtips.

***

The fighter Aces had become romanticised heroes of mechanised war. France and Germany in particular sought to hearten civilians weary of anonymous slaughter in the trenches by exalting a relative handful of pilots as symbols of individual (and national) bravery.

The propagandists trumpeted the young men as 'Knights of the Air' and 'The Cavalry of the Clouds'. Celebrities of their era, the pilots were lionised for supposed chivalry and the revival of individual duels in an age when soldiers lived under the perpetual threat of shells fired by distant and unseen gunners.

The reality, of course, was very different. Life for these pioneers of aerial combat was often 'nasty, brutish and short', in the words of the English philosopher Thomas Hobbes. For instance, the famous British pilot Mick Mannock was not alone in carrying a revolver to kill himself if his aircraft caught fire.

Chivalry faded quickly as the war ground on. Which fighter pilot living on his nerves would choose to fly head-on at an enemy—in a reckless echo of medieval jousting—if their combined four machine guns bridged the gap with some 40 bullets a second? Far better to heed the illustrated posters on the squadron walls, which showed them how to find the blind spot beneath an enemy, allowing a safe shot in the back. A successful aerial assassin lived to stalk again.

Idealistic Great War notions of war in the air were glamorised post-war by Hollywood, revived in WWII, and were most recently reinforced in *Top Gun, Pearl Harbour* and *Flyboys*. The globally syndicated *Peanuts* cartoon had a recurring storyline where Snoopy the beagle dreamed of his kennel as a Great War cockpit in a literal dogfight: 'Curse you, Red Baron!'

Given this near-universal appreciation of 'The Ace', how is it that Alec Little, Australia's most successful fighter pilot, is unknown to the general community?

Our national consciousness has been significantly shaped by Australia's military past, from Gallipoli to the Western Front, from the Rats of Tobruk to Long Tan and current conflicts. We respect, sometimes revere, military heroes: Simpson and his donkey at Gallipoli, the consummate Great War fighting soldier Albert Jacka, the inspirational Burma Railroad surgeon 'Weary' Dunlop and Olympian commanders like General Sir John Monash.

This revived interest in our military heritage was partly stimulated by the 'Australia Remembers' campaign commemorating the 50th anniversary of the end of WWII. The Dawn Service at Anzac Cove at Gallipoli on 25 April, an intensely emotional experience, draws more than 10,000 people, mostly young Australians.

The growing appreciation of the cost of three years of combat on the Western Front was heightened by the debate over the exhumation and partial DNA identification of almost 200 Australian Diggers, some of those killed in the 1916 Battle of Fromelles, the deadliest 24 hours in Australian history.

There was satisfaction in 2008 in closing a bitter chapter in naval history when a high-tech search discovered HMAS *Sydney* and its 645 dead, 67 years after the cruiser's disappearance off the coast of Western Australia after combat with the German armed raider *Kormoran*.

There has been a rash of books on the jungle combats on the Kokoda Track in Papua New Guinea, on Tobruk and El Alamein and more, which captured the deeds and memories of the fading WWII generation.

Given this resurgence in appreciation of our military heritage, and Australian admiration of its military heroes, why is Alec Little known only to Great War historians and aviation enthusiasts? At the start of the war the young man from the inner Melbourne suburb of Windsor, a commercial traveller for his father's book-importing business, was one of hundreds who had no luck volunteering for Australia's tiny air force. Determined to fight in the air, he paid his own fare to Britain in 1915, and a small fortune for flight training, before volunteering to join the Royal Naval Air Service (RNAS).

Alec Little was largely lost to history because he had to join a foreign service. He and his scores of flying colleagues who fought in British services were not even footnotes in early editions of the official Australian War Histories restricted to the achievements of Australian units.

His death at 22 ended an unsurpassed combat career and denied him possible post-war fame. Some of Australia's Great War pilots became aviation trailblazers—notably Sir Charles Kingsford Smith, Bert Hinkler and Sir Gordon (P. G.) Taylor—while others like Harry Cobby, Stan Goble, Adrian Cole and George Jones went on to high rank in the Royal Australian Air Force.

If it all seems so long ago, that Great War we usually see recalled in jerky black and white archival film footage, remember that one of Little's RNAS contemporaries survived to 2009. The true gulf is in the attitudes of the old Anglo-Australia firmly tied to the 'Mother Country'. Perhaps this search for Alec Little will give later generations a hint of some of the beliefs which led so many Australians to volunteer.

Alec Little lies in the gardened geometry of the small Commonwealth military cemetery at Wavans, northeast of Abbeville. A far-better-remembered flying hero lies a wingspan away—Britain's most highly decorated WWI Ace, James McCudden VC. The 44 graves here, softened by roses, bright splashes of gazania, lavender and other plantings, seem far removed from the evening rush of travellers to the Menin Gate memorial at Ypres in Belgium, where the local firemen play *Last Post* at 8pm nightly. Equally distant is the imposing marble architecture of the Australian National Memorial at Villers-Bretonneux, now the focus of an overseas Anzac Day commemoration second only to Gallipoli.

The politicians and Service chiefs and TV crews of multiple nations never go to the hillside cemetery at Wavans, surrounded by Pierre Geron's wheat and barley fields. The farmer occasionally sees groups visiting the cemetery. He once tried to comfort a crying young girl, asking if she had a family member there. 'I'm just praying for them,' she replied.

Who cries for Alec Little? He deserves wider recognition as a heroic individual, and a symbol of a lost generation.

Chapter 1
Between The Lines

Alec Little's generation knew 'Between The Lines' as the hazardous No Man's Land between opposing trenches. The Western Front's trenches stretched 700km from the Belgian coast to France's border with Switzerland.

Metaphorically, readers have long been reminded to 'read between the lines' to tease out messages not stated directly, for legal or other reasons.

Magazine serialisations used to introduce new chapters with a synopsis—'The Story So Far'—which typically concluded *Now Read On …*

'*Reading on*', in Little's case, is hampered by modest documentation, especially the few personal communications. Unless some lucky or dogged researcher turns up his long-lost final logbook, or more private documents, readers are free to make their own interpretations, and extrapolate from 'facts' which may present only a fraction, or one perspective, of the truth.

Take the love story between Alec Little and Vera Field. We know of only one communication between the young pilot and the pretty Dover girl he married in 1916. It is the field telegram she sent to his Western Front airfield in 1917 telling him of the birth of their son: *Alec arrived 20th March*. Two communications, perhaps, if you count her headstone inscription at Wavans Cemetery:

> His ever loving wife
> And little son Blymp
> Also his loving father.

Best to judge the depth of her affection by her actions. Vera made the confronting pilgrimage to his grave with its timber Celtic cross grave marker crafted by his squadron's mechanics, then the 20,000km voyage with young Alec to start a new life in Melbourne near his family. When the official stone headstone was erected, she paid to have the temporary wooden grave cross shipped to Australia. In 1978 her surviving children donated memorabilia to the Australian War Memorial and the Australian Defence Force Academy. The grave cross and Alec Little's medals have been displayed at the Memorial for decades. Since 2009 they have featured prominently in a Great War aviation exhibition, opposite a display on a more famous contemporary, Manfred von Richthofen, whose control column and a flying boot were souvenired by Australian troops after the Red Baron was shot down in 1918.

It is one of the ironies of Little's meteoric combat career that Richthofen, Germany's top-scoring Great War Ace with 80 victories, was given a formal military funeral by the Australian Flying Corps, including volleys fired above his grave. All we know of farewells to Australia's greatest Ace is a photo of fellow pilots by his grave.

Now read on … without necessarily interpreting everything through the perspective of a later century. Beware distortions of memory, time, propaganda, censorship, family pride, religious faith and more.

Reporting on death or wounds is an example. A Commanding Officer trying not to further distress a grieving family would often write some compassionate confection on the lines of 'he died bravely, with a bullet in the heart, facing the enemy.' Only the war poets, antiwar novelists and some historians would talk of the frothing agony of lungs destroyed by poison gas, disintegration by shellfire, and every possible degradation of body and spirit.

Alec's death wound was variously recorded as in the heart, through both hips, in the groin, and in the upper thigh. Some writers have speculated that he was shot by a rear gunner from a Gotha bomber: might it not have equally been what later generations would call 'friendly fire', a bullet from the ground?

In the jigsaw of Little paperwork, errors and colourful speculation are repeated. For instance, his crash site at Noeux appears in several major sources as 'Norviz'—which does not exist. In his logbook, inconsistent spelling and phonetic approximations sometimes make for confusing place names. He was hardly alone— Allied soldiers anglicised scores of Belgian and French place names. Ypres, for example, was usually spoken of as 'Wipers'.

The documents offer a choice of usage of his Christian names. He was variously called Robert, Bob, Alec and sometimes 'Rikki' by fellow pilots. For the sake of consistency I shall use Alec (as his wife called him) except in quoted references.

His surviving logbooks are a key resource, quite detailed by the standards of the time and certainly more informative than the terse summaries of the combat reports usually gathered by the intelligence officer immediately pilots landed, adrenalin still high. But they need interpretation against the tumult and confusion of combat; ego; the British 'stiff upper lip' understatement of the age, with its distaste of 'shooting a line' self-glorification, and likely self-censorship exercised in these open documents.

The entries can be teasing. For instance, his entry on 23 January 1916, on his first solo flight after joining the Royal Naval Air Service, mentions that he *went through some clouds*. Maybe that was his first experience of clouds, a meteorological delight? Or was he just grateful to emerge on the far side right side up, in the era before blind-flying instruments?

Pilots' memoirs can be self-serving or guarded; a Commanding Officer's written comments are often cautiously phrased; family tales or memorabilia may understandably preserve only favourable (or inflated) recollections of lost ones.

Witnesses are notoriously fallible, and propagandists highly selective, even inventive. Journalists blinkered by government censorship would be tempted to embellish pilots' deeds to boost both morale and sales. Alec was at least spared the war correspondents' alliterative nicknames of the second global war. With Australia's highest-scoring WWII Ace dubbed 'Killer'

Caldwell in headlines, Alec in that later war would had difficulty escaping a 'Lethal Little' tag.

The distorting prism of patriotism affected the mythmakers, whether comrades honouring a friend, post-war film directors inventing a new 'dawn patrol' cinematic genre, or religious and State leaders commemorating 'the glorious dead' who 'paid the supreme sacrifice'.

The frenzy of combat has always made for confused recollections or reportage. Add the third dimension of aerial combat, and witnesses are under even greater pressure. There's a famous Little story about his solo fight with 11 German aircraft on 7 April 1917, witnessed by observers at an artillery battery. Did he really choose to attack 11 opponents? Or did the dozen aircraft suddenly find themselves sharing the same patch of sky, with dramatic consequences?

The temptation of mythmaking was memorably put at the end of a John Wayne western, *The Man Who Shot Liberty Valance*. The young editor cried: 'This is the West, sir. When the legend becomes fact, print the legend.'

Alec's 'West'—the Western Front—was horrific enough. Those who lived or died there do not need legends or embellishment.

Now read on ...

Chapter 2
Age of innocence

The 'Year of Our Lord' 1895—to use a calendar convention of the time—brought little cheer to the Australians absorbed in the long Federation debates that would see them wrestle with compromises to craft a new nation from a collection of Colonies.

'Year of Our Lord' may be outdated usage now, but was certainly apt then. In 1901 more than 96 per cent of Australians described themselves as Christians.

But there were few other certainties early in the second century of British settlement of Australia. For many this was an era of great hardship, especially in Victoria when the speculative Land Boom of the 1880s collapsed into a depression in the early 1890s.

The year 1895 was also the start of what would be called the Federation Drought, which blighted much of the country between 1895 and 1902.

Not a particularly auspicious year for the birth on 19 July of Robert Alexander Little, second child of James Little, who lived at 8 Lennox St. in the inner eastern suburb of Hawthorn. James imported and sold medical books, initially from 430 Bourke St., Melbourne; moving in 1913 to Centreway, 263 Collins St. Alec Little came from a warrior and frontier heritage. The family was descended from the Little clan prominent in the Anglo-Scottish border wars and raids which ranged from the late 13th century to the end of the 16th century. The marauding horsemen were often called reivers, from an old English word meaning 'to rob'. The Littles rode from Dumfrieshire, close to the border on the Scottish side. They were plunderers or freedom fighters, depending on which side of the perpetually-troubled border you tried to make a living.

A Robert Little born in Dumfrieshire in 1828 emigrated to Ontario, Canada in 1847. He married Susanna Cross (born in Ontario, also of Scots descent) and became a farmer near Innisfil, which still had a whiff of the frontier. Innisfil is by Lake Simcoe, 80km north of modern Toronto.

The Littles had eight children. His two sons inherited his own sense of adventure and wanderlust, although they chose a rather warmer frontier in Australia. James emigrated to Victoria in 1888, aged 26. His younger brother, Dr William Clow Little, recently graduated as a physician and surgeon, aged 29, followed him in 1889.

The brothers scored well on Enterprise, but poorly on timing. 'Marvellous Melbourne' of the early 1880s, with its legacy of neoclassical buildings built on Gold Rush money, was to lose its smugness as the depression struck.

Tens of thousands of breadwinners left families to seek work interstate, some heading for the recent gold discoveries in the near-deserts of Western Australia. Thousands sailed as far as South Africa, another Dominion.

The Scots made major contributions to Australian life. Tens of thousands from the great diaspora triggered by the highland clearances and other hard economic times migrated to Australia.

In Victoria, they were prominent pioneers in the Western District from the late 1830s, hard men ('squatters') who made great fortunes in wool after displacing Aboriginal communities and adapting to a wildly variable climate. With their new country partly vanquished, they competed with each other to leave an architectural legacy of bluestone homesteads, including ostentatious mansions qualifying as 'Scottish Baronial'.

Other Scots, like James Little, built city businesses, recognised, if sometimes stereotyped, for hard work and thrift. Scots also became prominent in the political, academic and religious life of the city built on gold and wool.

At 30, James married Susan ('Susy) Smith, who had been born in the inner Melbourne suburb of Fitzroy. There had been no children from her first marriage, at 17, to Patrick Smith at Greymouth, New Zealand.

Susy was 36 when she married James at Carlton in inner Melbourne. Their children were Sylvia Clow Little, Robert Alexander Little, James Simcoe Little and Dorothy Ethel Little. The Littles first lived in the relatively affluent eastern suburb of Hawthorn, able to send their sons to fee-paying private (church) schools, initially Camberwell Grammar School, then Scotch College.

Some less fortunate Victorians living in poverty accepted the government's offer of small parcels of bushland to turn into farms. But the romantic 'bush ballads' of 'Banjo' Paterson and other poets rang hollow to soft city folk trying to wrest a living on poor land, which broke many, or at least enforced a brutal survival of the fittest.

James' brother, Dr Billy Little, also went bush, but was better equipped to thrive than most of the smallholders. He built a flourishing practice in the small northern Victorian wheat town of Warracknabeal. His long and lively correspondence with a former friend from medical school in Canada, Grace Ritchie, lives again in Margaret Gillett's *Dear Grace: A Romance of History*. (In April 1893 he told Grace that James had married: 'He has a nice home and a fat wife so he should be happy and warm during the winter.') Dr Little died in 1911.

For Melbourne's middle class, the Edwardian era after the end of the Federation Drought was relatively comfortable. Some 75 km of cable tram tracks served the inner city's ordered geometry of streets. By 1911 there were 2,722 cars amongst the horse-drawn vehicles.

On the world stage, Australians living on the edge of their vast continent had feared the foreign stranger since French navigators had competed with the British to explore much of the South Pacific, bequeathing many French place names to Australian maps. After the Crimean War of the 1850s, Russian expansionism into the Pacific prompted much construction of extensive coastal fortifications to protect Melbourne in the 1880s. Then the cartoonists' threatening

'Russian Bear' was replaced by the Yellow Peril, originally dating from racist assaults on Chinese miners on Australia's goldfields. This time the Peril was the Japanese, who had destroyed the Czar's Pacific fleet at Tsushima in 1905.

Australians, taking for granted the protection of the Royal Navy, would have watched with satisfaction as the tactical lessons of Tsushima—especially the need for single-calibre large guns, to avoid the targeting confusion of shell splashes from multiple calibre weapons—shaped the trend-setting design of the Royal Navy's all-big-gun *Dreadnought*. Its launch in 1906 made 'pre-Dreadnought' battleships obsolete, prompting the Germans into a 'Naval Race' to match the British technological leap.

For those concerned about Australia's defence, and who cared to look beyond romantic Boer War images of Australian bushmen galloping across the veldt, there were portents to future war in Japan's successful if costly siege of heavily entrenched and fortified Port Arthur in 1904–05. This was massacre by Maxim guns, 280mm German mortars, quick-firing artillery and hand grenades ... with use of searchlights, radio signalling, barbed wire and more.

The xenophobia enshrined in what was sometimes described as an Anglo-Australian culture was soon to be confirmed by the White Australia Policy with its immigration restrictions. Australians felt themselves under the protection of the British Empire. Alec and his schoolmates would have been quizzed on those large red patches on the schoolroom globe which represented British control over a quarter of the world's land and a quarter of world population. Although Queen Victoria had died in 1901 after reigning since 1837, her grandchildren dominated the Royal houses of Europe—surely a unifying force for civilisation? Never mind that Kaiser Wilhelm II of Germany was a nightmare for his diplomats, given to occasional outrageous and belligerent statements, and insisting on challenging British global naval supremacy. Surely the early 20th Century promised much as the technical revolutions rolled on? The Balkans might have been in turmoil again, but that seemed a way of life and death there ...

Echoes of the public celebrations for Federation on 1 January 1901 probably meant just another grown-ups party for five-year-old Alec Little. It's easy to imagine Alec and his young brother James playing soldiers to the adult background of newspaper reports of significant Australian involvement in the Boer War (1899–1902). Britain was initially humiliated by the two largely self-governing Boer Republics of the Transvaal and the Orange Free State.

Australians had fought abroad before in minor conflicts of Empire. This time the Colonies, and subsequently the new nation, contributed some 16,000 troops in Australian contingents, and another 7000 Australians in other colonial and irregular units. More than 600 Australians died in what ended as Australia's first military engagement as a nation.

Six Australians received Victoria Crosses. Australian war correspondents, including 'Banjo' Paterson, made much of Australian heroics at the Elands River and elsewhere.

With the greatly outnumbered Boers usually compelled to practice guerrilla warfare, conventions of correct military behaviour were at risk. Harry 'Breaker' Morant and Peter Handcock were charged with shooting civilians in reprisal for the death of a fellow officer. A British court martial ordered their execution by firing squad. This became the stuff of bitter legend, with cries of 'scapegoating' in an ugly war of irregulars that also saw tens of thousands of Boer civilians die of disease in 'concentration camps' created by the British to restrict the Boer commandos' ability to live off the land.

The 'Breaker' Morant scandal confirmed many Australians' suspicion about patronising British attitude to 'Colonials'. Australian governments refused to let British military courts apply the death penalty to Australian troops, something which would enrage Field Marshal Douglas Haig in the Great War.

The echoes of Boer War controversies were fading when a truly world-changing event took place on the bleak sand dunes at Kill Devil Hills on the coast of North Carolina in the USA. On 17 December 1903, the Wright Brothers made the first piloted, powered flight.

The new mass media made pioneering aviators the celebrities of the day; their epics were inevitably 'intrepid', if sometimes fatal. The leather-helmeted young men were a staple for mass-readership newspapers and magazines and early movie cameras. Portents here, too, with Louis Bleriot's flight across the English Channel in 1909 bypassing Britain's moat against European invaders, and the Royal Navy. Those military authorities willing to experiment with unreliable aircraft usually saw them purely as flying cavalry, 'eyes in the sky'. Credit for the first bombing raid is usually given to an Italian airman, Lt Giulio Gavotti, who dropped four hand grenades on a Turkish camp in Libya on 1 November 1911. No damage was reported.

Today, when we fly around the world diverted by the riches of entertainment systems, rarely bothering to look out a window, it's hard to appreciate the public wonderment of that era when flight was a poorly understood miracle of physics, performed in machines built of fragile materials with dubious design, by those who learned, or died, on the job.

In the 1890s Australian Lawrence Hargrave had made a key contribution to the theory of flight with his invention of box kites, structures adopted for the first successful flying machines. Electrical engineer John Duigan was determined to be the first Australian to fly an aircraft in Australia, even if he had to build it himself. He was doing exactly that, using his own design and construction and an engine made in Melbourne, on a family farm property at Mia Mia just northwest of Melbourne when fate condemned him to second place.

The American novelist Mark Twain, who memorably described Australian history as reading like 'the most beautiful of lies', would have appreciated the irony that Australia's first flight was not made by the local inventor, but the international showman and escapologist, Harry Houdini.

Houdini brought his Voisin aircraft to Digger's Rest, a hamlet just outside Melbourne, not far from where Duigan was labouring over wood, wires and fabric. On 18 March 1910 Houdini escaped not from a cell or sealed trunk, but planet earth, making Australia's first controlled, powered flight. Sixty years later Melbourne's international air terminal would be built nearby at Tullamarine.

Australians prefer winners. The unlucky Duigan was unable to take off until four months later, making the first flight in an Australian-designed and built aircraft on 16 July 1910. Today a replica of Duigan's craft hangs in the main foyer of Melbourne Museum, while the original, too fragile for display, rests in storage. Second place again.

Such adventures would particularly appeal to young boys. Alec Little's descendants recall family lore that says he was 'always keen on flying'. Then a 14-year-old schoolboy, Alec presumably saw the extensive newspaper coverage, including Houdini's flight of almost 10km in 7 minutes 37 seconds on 31 March.

Chapter 3

'The Bugles of England —and how could I stay?'

The old Anglo-Australia seems light years distant in cultural terms: a galaxy far away.

Yet the last Australian veteran of the Great War, Jack Ross, died in 2009 a few months ahead of British veteran, Henry Allingham, who had served in the Royal Naval Air Service and died at 112.

Two long lifetimes, but across a cultural gulf that would have been unimaginable for young Australians at school in the first decade of the 20th century.

There were 600 boys in the great bluestone hulk of Scotch College on Lansdowne St on Eastern Hill, central Melbourne. They were heirs to a stern Presbyterian tradition taught at the College from 1851. Doubt was not really an option. Teachers aimed to instil a strong faith and the compelling virtues of duty and love of country, which automatically included the 'Mother Country' and its Imperial task. There was a pervasive sense that all was right with the British world. (Britain's competitors for Empire would regard this as Imperial arrogance.)

Scotch College prepared upper and middle class boys for university. It became prominent among Australia's Public Schools. It aimed at a healthy mind in a healthy body, with various sports offered, including boxing. To escape the crowded asphalt yards, students crossed into the Fitzroy Gardens, part of the magnificent series of parks which are treasures of inner Melbourne. Such broad indoctrination was often characterised as 'muscular Christianity'.

Beyond the influences of school and family attitudes, what else might have helped shape Alec Little and his younger brother James Simcoe Little, and lead Alec to voyage halfway around the world to join what today's students might see as someone else's fight?

Newspapers and books were the information sources, as Australians did not enjoy radio broadcasts until the early 1920s. For instance, books by the English author Rudyard Kipling would be a standard in many homes boasting a modest library. Kipling was a 19th century celebrity, the poet laureate of Empire. Today he is usually characterised, if not reviled, as an ultra-imperialist, or perhaps vaguely recognised by youngsters as linked to Walt Disney's animation of *The Jungle Book*. His rousing tales and ballads from far-flung places presented exciting tales of duty, honour, sacrifice, 'the white man's burden' and 'dominion over palm and pine'. No surprise that Little's fellow pilots would give the young Australian the nickname 'Rikki', abbreviating the name of the lethal cobra-killing mongoose from *The Jungle Book*.

Australia produced its own Imperial storytellers, some with global sales. Teachers and parents moulding the minds of young Scotch students would have welcomed an international best seller from Melbourne, *Deeds That Won The Empire*. Never mind that it was written by a prominent Methodist clergyman, William Henry Fitchett, at a time of strong religious differences among the Christian denominations.

Fitchett's foreword promised that 'the tales here told are written, not to glorify war, but to nourish patriotism in these ease-loving days ... they represent an effort to renew in popular memory the great traditions of the Imperial race to which we belong'. This prolific writer, noted educator and passionate Imperialist had written a series of newspaper articles on highlights in British military history at the suggestion of a senior naval officer. In 1897 his tales of heroism were recycled into a book which sold more than 100,000 copies around the world.

Another international bestseller by a Melbourne author would not have been judged suitable character-forming reading for impressionable Scotch College boys. *The Mystery of a Hansom Cab,* by a barrister's clerk, Fergus Hume, was prominent among early crime novels. Hume described his 1886 book as a 'murder, a mystery and a description of low life in Melbourne'. Fitchett's book has vanished along with the Empire it glorified, while Hume's crime novel is still in print.

It was a time of 'ripping yarns', with pluck and derring-do ('daring deeds') the sales recipe exemplified by the large circulation of the *Boy's Own Paper* aimed at young and teenage boys. Published weekly in Britain from 1879, it reinforced patriotic attitudes with heroic tales of adventure for youth. Initially intended by the Religious Tract Society to encourage younger children to read, and to teach Christian morals, by the turn of the century it took aim particularly at British grammar school (independent school) audiences. This British institution lingered until 1967. You'll still hear the dismissive phrase 'Boys Own' applied to improbable adventures, jingoism and long-vanished attitudes.

Alec Little left little of a paper trail at school. He and his brother James came from Camberwell Grammar School to join Scotch College on 20 May 1907. The admission ledger notes that Alec had studied French—something that even in his wildest dreams of adventure he could not have imagined being useful a decade later on the far side of the world. Trawling the surviving Scotch College records indicates he was an average student at best. To borrow a term from cricket—a sport at which Australians were enjoying some success in combat with the 'Mother Country' following the birth of The Ashes competition in 1882—he didn't bother the scorer by appearing in the lists of prize winners and those who won lesser distinctions, roughly the top half of the class. The only recognition that we know of was a swimming medal.

He paid for boxing lessons in 1909, and learned basic military skills with the cadets between 1909 and 1911.

There's an apocryphal story of daredevil bravado there, walking along a wall parapet. (There would be a genuine cliff-hanger later on the White Cliffs of Dover.)

If Alec is a wraith in his school years, other influences that worked on him are obvious in the school magazine, *The Scotch Collegian*. It is chilling to revisit this long-gone Australia in the peace of the College archives, reading dusty copies from 1904 onwards, knowing the catastrophe to come that would result in the death of more than 200 former Scotch boys.

The former Scotch archivist, Dr Jim Mitchell, says that while the boys' enthusiastic magazine output was always under the guidance of a teacher, they had significantly more freedom than students contributing to other school magazines.

For most of the first decade of the 20th century, optimism prevailed. The cadets' notes (immediately following the Church Union copy) were generally in the vein of 'a jolly good time was had by all', even if they complained about the miserly few rounds each was permitted to fire on annual camp.

The cadet corps skirmished in the Fitzroy Gardens, picking up the rudiments of infantry movement in the open, as some brothers or fathers had learned the hard way in South Africa. Such skills were soon to be rendered largely irrelevant in trench warfare. Cadets even had access to a rifle simulator which allowing musketry practice without having to go miles to a rifle range, or waste expensive ammunition.

They were aware of the price of Empire, with at least seven Old Boys dead in the Boer War. 'Fighting for the Unity of the Empire', as Melbourne's Boer War memorial would eventually put it.

The College magazine tracks the nation's growing military preparedness, underlined by Field Marshal Kitchener's visit to advise the government in 1909. *The Defence Act 1909* made training and service compulsory in time of peace. Between 1911 and 1929 Australian males aged between 18 and 60 were required to perform militia service within Australia and its territories.

In 1907, the magazine's Cadet Notes noted 131 on the roll. The author sought more recruits, noting in part that 'a rifle exercise, such as fixing bayonets, appeals much more to a boy's interest than a manual exercise. Be that as it may, the time of compulsory rifle drill is at hand, so boys who are not now cadets will have to serve their time, whether they like it or not.'

In 1908 the Shooting column noted that a large number of cadets had recently gone through the musketry course prescribed for the Commonwealth Military Cadet Corps by the Defence Department. No polite fictions of bullseye targets; each cadet fired 20 shots from his Westley Richards rifle at targets representing a man's head and shoulders.

In 1910, the Cadet diarist said: 'We welcome compulsory military training, and are pleased to think that the compulsion will have to be applied to very few boys in Scotch College.'

The Scotch Collegian printed J. G. Smyth's *Alexander Morrison Essay*, 1910, 'The Defence of Australia.' Smyth, a student, asked if Australia could expect to achieve a great future 'by any other means than those by which all other great peoples have become powerful and rich—by forging the rungs of the ladder by which they have reached the summit of their power out of the swords and guns of conquered foes. A nation, history reminds us, can become great only by passing through the sad ordeal of a war.' He bemoaned the stumbling block of ever-present 'anti-militarism … this spirit is fortunately dying out, owing to the efforts of our statesmen in impressing on the people the necessity for defence.' John Gladstone Smyth was fortunate; he served in both world wars and died in 1971.

With war looming, Scotch's vice-captain in 1914, James Burns, wrote in the magazine of the student: 'Later he will look with pride and affection on the great brotherhood of Public Schools, all striving with a common aim towards a common end—the making of men for the Empire.' After school, 'patriotism for the Empire will succeed, though not replace, loyalty to the school'. During basic training before going overseas, Burns wrote a poem capturing the intense patriotism of the time. It became famous in school history, and known widely across Australia and the British Empire:

For England

> The bugles of England were blowing o'er the sea,
> As they had called for a thousand years, calling now to me;
> They woke me from dreaming in the dawning of the day,
> The bugles of England—and how could I stay?
>
> The banners of England, unfurled across the sea,
> Floating out upon the wind, were beckoning to me;
> Storm-rent and battle-torn, smoke-stained and grey,
> The banners of England—and how could I stay?
>
> O, England, I heard the cry of those that died for thee,
> Sounding like an organ-voice across the winter sea;
> They lived and died for England, and gladly went their way;
> England, O England, how could I stay?

Corporal Burns 'lived and died for England', shot in the head on 18 September 1915 on the arid peninsula called Gallipoli. 'He had a high sense of honour,' *The Scotch Collegian* noted in his obituary.

After leaving school, Boyd Thompson, editor of the school magazine in 1912, wrote:

To the Mother School

> Mother, thy blessing! the time has come
> To follow the rest of thy stalwart sons
> Forth, to the sound of the rolling drum,
> So soon to be lost in the roar of guns,
> Where the banner of Britain to glory runs.
> Mother, thy blessing! The time has come..."

… and more.

Sergeant Thompson died in action near Flers on the Somme on 10 November 1916.

'They were ultra-Imperialistic', Dr Mitchell wrote in the Scotch sesquicentenary history, *The Deepening Roar.* 'Scotch supported the war fiercely.'

The school principal added *Patriae*—For the Country—to the school motto in 1914. There were over 1230 enlistments from what was regarded as the second-largest public school in the Empire at the time. The 'Old Scotchies', as they called themselves, held reunions in faraway battlefields. These outliers of Empire would have agreed with the sentiment and fervour of Labor Party leader Andrew Fisher who declared on the outbreak of war in 1914 that 'Australians will stand beside our own to help and defend Britain to our last man and our last shilling.'

There are 204 names of the dead on the honour roll, the equivalent then of two graduating classes. For years it was a tradition for the Headmaster to intone the names of the dead on Remembrance Day; students would try to guess which name he would reach before his composure faltered. Continuing research by the archivists has added more names (and deleted one) from the toll, which in 2012 stood at 211 former students and five teachers.

David Merrett, writing on 'Scotch College In the Great War' in *Melbourne Studies in Education* in 1982, noted that 35 per cent of Old Boys became officers, and 23 per cent NCOs. 'The character of the school plays an important part in the explanation of this rush to the colours ... the undiluted Calvinism preached at the school during prayers, and practised in the classroom, examination hall and on the playing fields, prepared the boys spiritually, mentally and physically for the rigours of war. They knew where their duty lay ...'

The school magazine quickly reflected the anti-German bitterness which saw scores of Australian towns renamed, some internments, and many of German descent obliged to report routinely to the authorities. An example:

> Our new Kindergarten alphabet books may run something like this—

A was an Allemand who went out to slay

B the brave Belgians who stood in his way;

…

G were the Germans, once men of good fame.

H were the Huns which they quickly became.

I's the Imperial bully and boss,

J is John Bull who gave him a toss…

… and so on.

The mythmaking started early. The *Collegian* editorialised in August 1915 about 'our admiration for the deeds of the Australian troops … and the glory of their achievements. They have definitely established themselves as one of the most formidable and dangerous armies of the world … most armies are noted either for their extreme recklessness or for their dogged bravery. The Australians combine both these qualities with a kind of cool and nonchalant humour in the face of fire, which is peculiar to them, and them alone.'

It concluded: 'To be killed on the battlefield is the most magnificent death, and the school is proud to think that many of her sons have thus died.'

Little left Scotch on 5 July 1912, at the end of second term. He and his brother James worked as commercial travellers for their father, a less than enthralling job marketing titles like *Practical Gynaecology: a manual for students and general practitioners* by George Horne (James Little, Melbourne. Stillwell & Co 1911). The young men presumably 'minded the shop' in 1914 when their father and his oldest child, Sylvia Clow Little, sailed to Canada on the *Niagara*. They arrived at Vancouver on 21 July, 23 days after Archduke Franz Ferdinand of Austria had been assassinated at Sarajevo. Presumably they called on Canadian relatives. There may have also have been a minor family drama playing out against the background of nations stumbling towards the first global conflict. Dr James Webb was attending Sylvia's ill mother in 1915. In March 1916, Sylvia, aged

22, would marry Dr Webb, 42, whose divorce had been granted the previous month. Perhaps the voyage had been in part James' attempt to sever a relationship seen as unsuitable.

The Little brothers would soon quit salesmanship for war. According to family tales, Little was fired with patriotism and was desperately anxious to see action before the war was over. But as one of his descendants emphasises, the lure of being involved in aviation was a key motivation. Rather than just go to the nearest Army recruiting depot, as his young brother James had done, Alec went to considerable trouble (and expense) to overcome the barriers that appeared to bar his way to becoming a pilot. His father is reported to have paid for his P&O fare to Britain, and his flight training.

Chapter 4
'The Progress of Madness'

Most passengers boarding the P&O Royal Mail Ship *Malwa* at Melbourne on 27 July 1915 would have appreciated the fine and very pleasant winter day, with light winds and a maximum of 17 degrees.

The Little family had other things on their mind. They farewelled Alec only a month after his younger brother James Simcoe Little, 18, had sailed on the troopship *Wandilla*, a 14th Battalion (6th Reinforcement) bound for Gallipoli. Gallipoli was emerging as a national tragedy. The casualty lists were numbing the nation. Soldiers' families trembled at the approach of a telegram boy, their local clergyman or other potential bearer of the worst tidings.

At least one report—the London *Daily Mail* of 23 June, 1917—states that Alec's father sent him to England to attend an aviation school. Alec faced a potentially hazardous voyage, then the high-risk hazards of learning to fly, only 12 years after the Wright Brothers pioneered powered flight. If he survived training—and thousands across Europe did not—he would face equally brave young men with different insignia on their aircraft.

His father James had an additional burden. His wife Susy, 59, had been ill for almost two years with breast cancer and a secondary cancer of the liver. Her condition would not necessarily have been obvious to her children. Given the reticence of the age, and a likely reluctance to burden sons who were confronting their own mortality, it is possible she concealed her illness.

Malwa offered a comfortable ride to war. The 5,900-tonne steamship completed in 1908 was one of the M-class vessels, the pride of P&O's fleet. She had token armament: the British Admiralty had long had a say in construction of ships likely to be taken into service in future conflict. Some decks were strengthened to carry guns to be installed on declaration of hostilities.

By now most German commerce raiders like the cruiser *Emden*—beached on Cocos Island in the Indian Ocean after combat with HMAS *Sydney* in November 1914—had been cleared from the seas. *Malwa's* service as a fast Royal Mail Ship meant that she usually sailed alone, avoiding slower convoys and relying on speed to escape U-boats.

Alec could expect around five to six weeks of relative boredom, compounded by frustration at the delay at moving between the Heaven of Australia and the Hell of world war. The voyage was interrupted by brief stops at romantic places which brought a sense of the exotic (if not Imperial superiority) to those going Home, as people said then. In some ports, local children would dive for pennies thrown from the ship by passengers. There would be haggles with shopkeepers, unease about confrontation with beggars, and fear of foreign foods, water and disease.

After calling at Sydney/Melbourne/Adelaide/Fremantle, the mail steamers usually crossed the Indian Ocean to Colombo in Ceylon (Sri Lanka), continuing via Aden on the Red Sea, the Suez Canal, Port Said in Egypt and on to Marseilles in France, where some passengers would take train services. Royal Mail Steamers usually continued via Gibraltar and Plymouth to London.

Sailing the Mediterranean towards the end of what must have seemed an interminable voyage, the entertainments officer organised a Grand Evening Concert on 31 August, starting on the second saloon deck at 8.15.

The programme noted that it was:

'In aid of the Mine Sweepers Fund':
Greater Love hath no man than this,
That a man lay down his life for his friends.

'R. A. Little' appeared fourth on a 13-part programme, reciting 'The Progress of Madness.' Five performances were billed as 'humorous'; Alec's contribution was the only one with any potential resonance to the chaos which had followed the world's stumbling into war the previous August.

'The Progress of Madness' was presumably drawn from T. Houston's very long poem of the same name, an 1802 English satire (anthologised as late as 1908) attacking an legal injustice which had seen a man committed to a 'mad-house' instead of jail, for a minor offence. A couplet gives the flavour: 'Justice has at length become/Not only blind, but deaf and dumb.'

We don't know whether Alec was a concert volunteer, or conscript—if 'The Progress of Madness' had been assigned to him, or if he chose it with ironical intent after seeing the Edwardian Era certainties, the imperatives of Civilisation and Empire, imperilled by the assassination at Sarajevo.

Notwithstanding the adrenalin rush of his performance, one hopes that he ruthlessly edited Houston's defence of the rights of man. Especially since Part 1 runs to 432 lines, and Part 2 is even longer.

The Grand Concert concluded with 'God Save The King'. A few days later the young Australian landed in England, bound for the grass airfield at Hendon in northwest London to check out the flying schools.

Malwa sailed on, and survived the war.

Chapter 5
Surviving training

The small biplane buzzes out of the early morning mist over Port Phillip Bay, descending over the hangar dented by Captain Tommy White's Bristol Boxkite in a misjudged landing on 11 September 1914.

It lands neatly on the grass airfield at Point Cook, west of Melbourne. It rocks slightly as the pilot jumps out, goggles in hand, to return to earth.

Reality check. This is 2008, although if filmed in black and white, the scene could easily suggest flickering footage from a Great War documentary, or interwar Hollywood movies like *Wings* or *Dawn Patrol*, which established a genre and romanticised the Ace into the swashbuckling icon of 20th century warfare.

In August 1914, four Army officers arrived at this former sheep station by Port Phillip Bay, 25km southwest of the Victorian capital of Melbourne. Pioneers of Australian military aviation, they spent three months at the Central Flying School at Point Cook. Richard Williams went on to fight in the Middle East with the Australian Flying Corps and his post-war rise through the ranks would earn him the title of 'The Father of the Royal Australian Air Force' (RAAF).

One of his three colleagues at Point Cook, Tommy White, would be captured in Mesopotamia while flying with a small Australian unit. He wrote of his escape from the Turks in *Guest of the Unspeakable*. Elected to Federal Parliament in 1929, the Melbourne businessman served for 22 years, known as a loyal Imperialist and fighter for the rights of ex-servicemen. His WWII tasks included working as liaison officer with the RAF in London. He served as Australian High Commissioner to Britain from 1951–56 and was knighted in 1952.

Alec Little was among the unsuccessful hundreds who had sought to be among Australia's first military aviators. Almost a century after his fruitless application, RAAF Base Williams, Point Cook, is Australia's most important aviation heritage site. It was placed on the National Heritage List in 2007 after being saved from housing development by a public campaign which saw it remain in government ownership. Some 100,000 people annually visit the RAAF Museum. Its collection includes one of its original aircraft, a 1914 Maurice Farman Shorthorn biplane. There are regular flying demonstrations of some of the museum's historic aircraft and a replica Sopwith Pup.

This is also a civilian airfield. Two de Havilland Tiger Moth biplanes offer the excitement of open-cockpit flight, totally removed from the sterile airline experience. These Moths, built in the early 1940s, are survivors of the 7,000-plus sturdy basic trainers which trained generations of British and Australian air force pilots. Starting at $120 for a 20-minute joyride, you experience the wind in your face, and a real sense of the elements.

Point Cook was founded in 1913 only 10 years after the Wright Brothers flew. It is one of the oldest continuously operating military airfields in the world, although RAAF basic training has been done elsewhere since 1993.

Back in 1914, the orderly officer would step outside for a daybreak ritual, holding his handkerchief up by a corner. If it fluttered in the breeze, the aircraft stayed in the hangars until the wind eased, and the students headed for classrooms (especially learning theory of flight, and meteorology) or the workshops where they learned the innards of the Box-kite's 50-horsepower Gnome rotary engine.

Learning to fly in aviation's infancy was a frequently lethal ambition. Airframes were primitive, the science poorly understood, instructors varied widely, and reliable engines were a lottery. For many, 'going solo' was one of the most exhilarating of life's experiences; for quite a few, the last of life's experiences.

The good news was that poor landings, or controlled crashes, occurred at relatively slow speeds. There was a hoary joke about 'a good landing is one you can walk away from'.

The alternative was a devil's list of evil endings rarely mentioned in stirring tales of heroic aviators. Sudden deceleration might crush your face against the front of the cockpit. You might be impaled on a broken ash strut, or lashed by the metres of wire which had previously held your aircraft together. Death by fire was especially feared. Many lived with the secret dread of having their machine disintegrate around them: from 1,000ft, you had perhaps five seconds of freefall terror before the adventure finished; from 5,000ft, perhaps 30 seconds of nightmare.

While young men with dreams of duty or glory may have convinced themselves that death was for others, for thousands of pilot trainees in the Great War the reality was an abrupt and messy departure, unhelpful to the morale of other trainees. All this before you saw an enemy.

***

In London it seems likely that Alec found that a civilian flying licence was the best ticket to a Service career, as the Royal Flying Corps (RFC) and RNAS usually accepted as volunteers only those with flying licences. At Hendon, he had to choose between five flying schools: Grahame-White, Beatty, Ruffy-Baumann, Hall and London & Provincial. He (or his father) paid a hundred pounds— roughly $10,000 in today's dollars—for what now seems very basic training. While the former busy airfield has long closed, Hendon is now the site of the Royal Air Force (RAF) Museum, a memorial and major attraction attracting 300,000 thousand visitors annually.

One of the civilians Alec met during his training would join him in the RNAS. Squadron Leader Leonard Rochford, DSC and Bar, DFC left a vivid account of sink-or-swim flying tuition at London & Provincial in his autobiography *I Chose The Sky*. He had selected L&P because it was the only company which did not use dual control, preferring to have the pupil alone in the machine, and get him into the air by stages, giving him verbal instructions from the ground. 'I am sure it inspired more confidence in the pupil,' Rochford recalled. 'After all, the pioneers taught themselves to fly, flying was very much in its infancy and even instructors still had a lot to learn.'

The proprietors, Billy Warren and Geoff Smiles, recommended 'digs' at Mr Michael's guesthouse, *Hatherley*, near the aerodrome, shared by about a dozen pupils. Just as at Point Cook in faraway Victoria, there was no flying in the Caudron GIIIs widely used for flight training if there was the slightest breeze.

If his voyage on *Malwa* had exposed Alec to novel experiences, Hendon surely eclipsed it. Even before takeoff, he would become familiar with the reek of burned castor oil used to lubricate rotary engines (it would nauseate some pilots, including Little); perhaps varnish on a newly replaced strut, and the tang of dope, the highly flammable lacquer applied to tauten the fabric.

Training started with 'rolling'—taxying in a straight line, 'not as easy as you might think', Rochford reported. Little would have fastened his seat belt and listened with great concentration to the instructor. Between his legs was the control column or 'joystick' as it was usually called. You moved this backward or forward to make the machine ascend or descend by raising or lowering the elevators. Pushing it left warped the right wing and the machine banked left, and vice versa. The pilot's feet rested on a rudder bar connected to the vertical rudders above the tail plane, which steered the aircraft to left or right.

When the aircraft was 'rolling', the pilot would keep it moving forward by 'blipping' a switch on and off, controlling the 35hp 3-cylinder Anzani radial engine.

The next stage was 'straights'—a short flight across the aerodrome, a couple of yards (metres) above the grass. 'It felt rather like learning to ride a bike or horse, liable to lose one's balance and fall at any moment,' Rochford wrote. The third stage was to fly a half circuit, landing on the far side and returning in a straight flight. The fourth and final stage was a complete circuit of the aerodrome at 300 feet. That done, the tyros were judged capable of taking their 'ticket' test before an umpire.

On October 7, Rochford had to fly the first prescribed set of five figures of eight; then land within the required distance of 50 yards from a point near the centre of the aerodrome. The whole process was repeated. 'Then I ascended for the final 'Volplane' test and climbing to the stipulated 300ft I switched the engine off and descended (volplaned) to make a landing before switching on again.' Rochford passed, and received the Royal Aero Club Aviator's Certificate No 1840; as soon as he reached his 19th birthday he applied to the Admiralty for a Commission in the RNAS and soon after attended a Selection Board. 'Among other questions, the Board asked me about my Hendon flying course. I do not know whether the fact of getting my 'ticket' influenced their decision, but, after passing my medical test, I was accepted as suitable for training as an officer in the RNAS. Early in December I was sent to Greenwich for vaccination and inoculation.'

Little received certificate No 1958 on 27 October 1915 and followed a similar path to that of Rochford.

There's far more life in the pilot's certificate portrait of a young Alec glowering at the photographer than in the later formal uniformed images, resolute poses ideal for the family mantlepiece at 'Ryde', 113 Punt Rd., Windsor, Melbourne.

Here he is in civilian clothes, helmet in hand, in front of a Caudron. Surly? Arrogant? Pugnacious? He looks like a young Colonial who might not suffer fools, or British Senior Officers, gladly—a trait common to many of his countrymen building an ANZAC tradition of disrespect to authority, especially British authority.

Maybe he was enduring the laxative after-effects from the hot castor oil fumes from the rotary engine? But if you suspect a hint of Bad Attitude, you're right. The 20-year-old would soon push the patience of his senior officers at the RNAS, taking him to the edge of expulsion.

Barely two weeks after his graduation, there was hard news from home. His mother Susy had died on 15 November.

More drawn-out suffering, but on a national scale, ended on 20 December, when Australia's share of the multinational Gallipoli tragedy concluded with the last thousands of ANZACs somehow evacuated without loss of life. The evacuation and its elaborate deception measures were the only high points of a mismanaged campaign costing 8,141 Australian lives.

By now, Alec may have been aware that his young brother James had survived Gallipoli. Dysentery, with its persistent diarrhoea, had been the scourge of many armies in history, and in the unhygienic conditions of Gallipoli was almost as big a threat as the Turks. James fell victim and was evacuated to Egypt in August.

James was hardly the 'big bronzed Anzac' of legend; he was only 5 ft 4in (1.62m) tall, and weighed 10 stone (63.5kg). The medico examining him on enlistment noted 'fair complexion, grey eyes, brown hair', but did not pick up—or chose not to pick up?—that those grey eyes suffered myopic astigmatism. Short-sightedness was not recommended for a man trying to aim a .303 Lee Enfield rifle in a kill-or-be-killed situation.

James concealed the condition, and the examiner may not have been too fussy, intent on passing as many recruits as possible. The doctors in Egypt rated it 'a pre-enlistment condition', and he was discharged and returned to Australia in 1916, 'permanently unfit for service'. James senior was proud of his son's Gallipoli service. In 1918 he told the Melbourne *Herald* that James had fought at Lone Pine, another dread name in Australian military history.

By the end of 1915, there was no sign of an end to the world conflict. Officers would make sure that the Christmas Truce of 1914, which saw some brief fraternisation between opposing forces on the Western Front, would not be repeated. The propaganda services worked to ensure that 'The Beastly Hun' (you had a wide choice of chauvinistic epithets) was to be hated, not regarded in a moment of weakness as just another young man freezing in a hole in the ground, an easy rifle shot to the east.

This was the world that Alec Little prepared to enter after his last Christmas as a civilian.

Chapter 6

'His Commission will be terminated...

'Has a trick of landing outside the aerodrome'

On 14 January 1916, the 20-year-old who had paid his own way to the war was granted a commission as Temporary Probationary Flight Sub-Lieutenant Royal Naval Air Service. His first posting was to the Eastchurch Naval Flying School on the Isle of Sheppey, in Kent on the Thames Estuary. The Navy was reputed to demand more of its pilots in training than the RFC, with obvious benefits when they reached the Front.

Alec's surviving logbooks note the multiple technical perils faced by pilots in that era of fragile and often poorly designed aircraft driven by underpowered and temperamental engines. Northern European weather, enemy pilots and 'archie'—the British pilots' slang for anti-aircraft fire—merely compounded the hazards. No wonder that sensible pilots navigated from one possible emergency landing field to the next.

These were young men; one of the Royal Flying Corps recruitment posters promised a 'college to cockpit' adventure.

In an undated early notebook, Alec made brief remarks on engine details and flight instructions. He sketched carburettors and an early aircraft. Later he made model aircraft. He also listed addresses of people in Canada and Australia, and—the only reference to religion that is known—wrote a six-page summary of the first Book of Samuel from the Old Testament.

Nobody ever called Alec Little a gifted flier. His potential as a superb combat pilot was not yet in evidence as he slowly built up his hours with the RNAS. His logbooks record escapes from many potential disasters, mostly the fault of the machine, not the man.

Join him on his meteoric career with the RNAS and Royal Air Force. Logbook quotes are italicised.

Alec's first RNAS flight (23 January) was in a Caudron training aircraft with an instructor. Then—*Same day (flight by myself). Went through some clouds.*

Was this his first time in cloud? Pilots with only primitive instruments feared becoming dangerously disoriented in heavy cloud. They were especially wary of anything resembling cumulonimbus, a thunderstorm cloud. Only later, in combat, would they learn that clouds could be friend, not foe: they would learn to stalk an enemy from cloud.

On February 1 Alec was flying a Maurice Farman Shorthorn, an antiquated training aircraft which closely resembled the Wright Flyer, when he made the first of many forced landings: *switch got caught in sleeve and engine stopped, made a good landing in a field, got a soldier to start my prop & got away alright ...*

He faced double jeopardy that day. On a second flight, the engine stopped and he tried to 'V.P' (volplane, or glide) to the aerodrome but side-slipped on turning and had to land in a field near the aerodrome. *Made a good landing, there was no wind when I left and on coming down there was a wind blowing 25 miles an hour, this no doubt put me out in my judgement.* (An adjacent scrawl of 'Bad judgment' looks like an instructor's verdict.)

Seven days later, an engine pipe on a Maurice Farman Longhorn came off and *he had to land in small aerodrome ... got machine fixed.* On February 10 he climbed a Curtiss trainer to 11,800 ft *and could not get any higher ... the air was cold but I was quite warm inside the bus.* Especially in the northern European winter, pilots would don a wide variety of clothing to ward off frostbite in their open cockpits. Some resembled Polar explorers more than aviators. On the other hand, the white silk scarf often favoured by pilots was not for warmth or sartorial flair, but protection, as woollen scarves would chafe as pilots continually turned their heads to spot threatening aircraft.

With a grass airfield, and in winter, simply getting off the ground was not always straightforward. Three days later he *got wheel stuck in mud and had to be lifted out. Just was leaving & wheels sank in swampy ground, nearly stood down. Chip prop. Started off again but engine was missing and I came down again.*

February 16 brought a reminder of how aviation has always been weather-sensitive: *Started raining so came down.* In conditions of poor visibility, goggles smeared by rain and possibly engine oil were an added risk.

Alec notched up another forced landing on February 19 in a Maurice Farman Shorthorn: *gudgeon pin broke and connecting rod smashed cylinder walls & crank case. Made a good landing just outside flying ground.*

On February 20 he cut the petrol to his Bristol, but could not restart the engine, so landed in a field. A day later he noted a *joy ride with Mr Alcock.* If the young Australian was piloting, Mr Alcock was a brave man, or was not aware of Alec's growing tally of damaged aircraft. Then again, Flight Lieutenant John Alcock, an instructor at Eastchurch, was to prove a very brave man in 1919, piloting a Vickers Vimy in the pioneering non-stop crossing of the Atlantic, with Lieutenant Arthur Brown as navigator.

February 21 saw the worst battle of the war to that date start near Verdun in eastern France as Germany launched an attrition campaign that would last 10 months, become a byword for mass slaughter, and haunt France for decades.

On that day, Alec flew a Short: *Very bumpy machine. Glad to get down again, did not like the feeling of flying so slow. Made a good landing.* Two days later, the unpopular Short was *very steady but rolled very much with the least gust of wind, felt peculiar flying at 40mph.*

Two days later he was unhappy with a Bleriot, designed by the Frenchman who became a celebrity with the first Channel flight in 1909: *This machine flies left wing down, which took all my time to hold it up.* This was not the last time he would wrestle with an aircraft! Later that day the crankshaft on a different Bleriot broke. Too low to make the correct approach into the wind, he landed side on and bent a wheel.

Next day he *had a sham fight with another machine* in a lumbering Maurice Farman Shorthorn. This is his first known reference to the ultimate purpose of his training—to use his aircraft as a gun platform, and to kill. On February 28 he was obviously pleased with his Bleriot, and his emerging skills, after another sham fight: *got under its tail for quite a long time, made some very fine turns. Engine was not running very well so came down and found that a cylinder was blued* (heat-affected, threatening engine seizure). 'Under the tail' was a recommended blind spot. From there you could fire safely. Gallantry, chivalry and good sportsmanship did not come into it: aerial assassination was more the aim.

Alec did not impress his squadron commander, who noted in a confidential report of 6 March: 'As a pilot he is variable, usually flying well & plucky, but occasionally is very erratic. *Has a trick of landing outside the aerodrome* [my italics]. Has done about 19 hours ... as an officer he is not very good, & has a bad manner. Is generally fairly satisfactory; not good at theoretical work. Recommend him for seaplanes.' Alec was posted to Felixstowe Air Station on March 7.

Seaplanes? These young men dreamed of combat in the embryonic single-seat fighters of the day, not lumbering seaplanes. Two days after his senior's recommendation, Little was introduced to a twin-engined Curtiss America: *first trip in a seaplane, not as nice as land machines, too slow and too big, very slow in answer(ing) the controls.* A family legend—'He didn't like seaplanes!'—was born. 'Seaplanes' referred both to aeroplanes fitted with floats, and flying boats like the Curtiss America, which landed on their hull.

On March 21, Alec did his first patrol in a seaplane. He may have found some irony in the fact that it was April Fool's Day when he piloted a Curtiss America on the first patrol listed in his logbook, 3hr 10 mins to the Kentish Knock, off the Kent and Essex coasts. He and his gunner Hobbs were *armed with Lewis gun (four trays) and revolver (20 rounds)*. What you would do with a revolver is not clear. Four days later, he and pilot Railton practised another combat skill, bomb dropping, in a Short. On their second bombing practice that day, an engine failed.

On April 7, there was a sense of achievement in his entry: *First solo on America, got along alright.* That satisfaction lasted only two days: during a patrol in the large seaplane, the port engine began to miss. Little sighted some trawlers and landed alongside them. *On landing starboard engine moved in its bed and prop hit side of boat and broke, hitting the port engine and then going through top plane. Fire off red Very's light* (flare gun) *and* (a trawler) *picked us up. We were handed over to ML46* [motor launch] *& towed to Grain. We returned by train.*

Over three years he would show considerable initiative and variety in arranging transport back to his airfield after abandoning yet another bent aircraft.

Alec's next mishap was medical, not mechanical. On 17 April he was admitted to Shotley hospital with rubella (measles). He was discharged after 10 days. While he was in hospital, his commanding officer wrote a blunt second confidential report: 'As an officer he is quite hopeless & likely to remain so. As a Pilot he displays considerable courage and keenness, although somewhat lacking in skill. Apparently he would prefer to fly land machines. I think he could be made use of as an aeroplane pilot at Dunkerque, or some other front. I do not think it would be of any advantage to this Station for him to remain here.' He had obviously left senior officers in no doubt about his dislike of seaplanes!

On May 5 there was an even more pungent verdict: 'This officer has been reported on unfavourably & he is to be informed that if a further adverse report is received, his Commission will be terminated. You are to forward a report as to his progress and ability on 8th June 1916.'

On May 9, Alec was posted to Dover, where the RNAS duties included Channel reconnaissance, and intercepting possible German bombers. A senior officer must have read the riot act to the disgruntled Australian. Alec got the message. From being on the verge of disgrace—having possibly crossed the world for nothing—there was a remarkable turnaround:

Confidential Report, June 9:

> Has conducted himself satisfactorily. Has an amount of pluck & is extremely hardworking. As soon as he learns to be less irresponsible, & when flying to use his head to better advantage, I shall feel confident that he will do exceptionally well on Active Service.

The young Australian discovered an exciting world outside his aviation learning curve. The people around Dover welcomed the pilots, especially those from overseas. Alec met a pretty Dover girl, Vera, only child of Frank Field, a ship's steward, and his wife Ellen. The services often disapproved of junior officers getting married, fearing that family responsibilities might encourage caution in action. His courting of Vera might have been part of Alec's problems with his superiors.

In later life, Vera would describe Alec as being 'of average height, well proportioned, with hazel eyes which appeared forever alert. His movements, too, were quick and decisive and were made without waste of energy. He also had a sense of humour which his photographs belie.' A pilot colleague couldn't resist a pun, describing him as 'Little by name and stature'.

While at Dover he had demonstrated a different kind of courage which became part of the family saga. His obituary in *The Times* on 24 July 1918 concluded: 'His entire lack of fear was well evidenced at Dover immediately before crossing to France. A Royal Flying Corps pilot flew into Dover cliffs on a foggy day and crashed ... Little scaled down the cliffs and rescued the pilot.' In the 1930s Vera wrote 'he certainly did risk his life, and the life of the young pilot who flew into the cliff would not have been saved, for he was just about done, when my late husband reached him.' Vera added that there was talk of a recommendation for a lifesaving medal until people heard he had gone down the cliff again on the following day searching for seagull eggs—making light of the hazard involved.

More engine perils. On May 14 the engine of his Avro stopped. He landed with the wind and ran into a ditch, breaking chassis and prop and suffering slight shock and concussion. He continued to pile up repairs for the mechanics. Five days later, another engine stoppage: this time he landed in a small field, hit a fence, and broke the propeller and a strut. He was definitely not helping the war effort.

During a climbing test in a Curtiss on May 18 he showed an inquisitiveness that might not have been welcomed by his seniors. *Saw an aeroplane come down in a field, I came down and landed to see what was wrong and lost my prop. Later on a Bristol Bullet passed over & it also landed. We were unable to start the engines again and waited until a car came for us. We got away alright.*

By now he had 42 hours 41 minutes total flying time: his luck held until May 26, when he ran his Bleriot into a Nieuport Scout on landing.

How the wreckage piled up! June 9 saw him in serious trouble in a Curtiss: *Got lost in Thunder Cloud had no compass and could not find my way. Engine gave out and had to land on the beach at Hythe. Broke prop. Machine dismantled and towed to Dover.*

On 30 June he was posted to No 1 Wing operating from Dunkirk in France. Not without incident: leaving Dover for Calais and Dunkirk on 29 June in Bristol Scout No 1260, he *got turned over by the wind and wrecked the machine.*

The fate of Flight Lieutenant Talbot that day rammed home the basic rule of not attempting to return to the airfield if you got in trouble soon after takeoff. Talbot left in a Nieuport. His engine began to miss and he tried to turn back, stalling on the turn and nosediving onto the Dover road. Pilot and observer died.

Little had further problems later that day. His poor pre-flight check failed to spot that Bristol Scout No 3043 had no compass. He noticed a petrol pipe leak en route—with petrol leaks a nightmare in the days before parachutes—and would have been greatly relieved to have finally made it to Dunkirk.

The wait was over. Alec's shooting war was imminent. His flying time before active service was 119hr 20 min. He had survived at least 15 forced landings with only one admitted case of mild concussion. He also suffered stomach and eye trouble in the air from the castor oil fumes of rotary engines.

Chapter 7

Takeoff: Year of Killing, 1916

'A brilliant lone hand'

The propagandists of the major Western Front combatants, France and Germany, welcomed the air combat which developed quickly from the early days of pilots firing rifles or revolvers at each other. Nations competed to refine single-engine scouts firing one or more machineguns through the propeller arc, with devices linked to the camshaft (usually) interrupting the bullet stream when the propeller was in line with the muzzle.

The daily attrition in the trenches, or heavy losses from attacks inevitably defeated by the technological superiority of the defence, made poor copy for the handful of correspondents allowed near the Front. The correspondents seized on the young pilots, making romantic medieval allusions about the Knights of the Air. They wrote of them jousting in single combat, with a whiff of chivalry built in to turn the best of them into demigods. It was a return to the supposed good old days when a man's survival depended largely on his skills, not random death from a faraway artillery battery. Their off-duty celebrations also made for good copy, with the hard-living playboy Frenchmen Charles Nungesser and Jean Navarre especially flamboyant.

There were some gallant gestures, individual challenges made and respect paid to fallen opponents. Celebrities during their often short lives, the pilots were lionised in newspapers and illustrated magazines, films, and postcards. The title Ace usually conferred for five victories gave heroic status. Manfred Von Richthofen, greatest of them all, ordered a trophy cup from a Berlin jeweller for each victory. He died after 80 victories, his fame ensuring that the circumstances of his death are still debated by historians. There is a strong case that the single bullet which killed him was fired not by another pilot, but by a Digger with a machinegun.

Richthofen at least died quickly and cleanly. You can see another reality in photographs, usually suppressed at the time so as not to disturb morale or offend sensibilities. A charred corpse in a tangle of wire, blackened timber and engine. British onlookers gawking at the outline of a Zeppelin crewman's body impressed deep in his corner of a foreign field.

On July 1, Alec patrolled between Nieuport and Dixmude. It was the greatest day of slaughter in British military history, with almost 20,000 British soldiers killed as the Somme offensive was launched.

On July 9, his Bristol Scout 3043 was attacked near Ypres by a Fokker monoplane *which dived at me from above and behind. The H [hostile] machine fired all tracers or about 1 in 2. I turned right and he also turned right side slipping badly. We both did about six circuits, I was the inside man. The hun then broke away and I fired a tray [Lewis gun magazine] at him. While I was changing trays he attacked me again...and fired about 50 shots. He then passed in front of me about 20yds away still diving and I fired at him and saw my tracers enter the fuselage also saw one hit the engine. The machine nosedived and pulled out of it at about 1,000ft and glided east. I followed him down and saw him land in a field about 2 miles on his side of the lines.* (This is not on his official list of claims.)

On that occasion Little was caught from behind and above. Newcomers to air combat often described it as a whirling confusion, chaos which might suddenly end—if you were fortunate—when you found yourself apparently alone in a hostile sky, your heartbeat easing. The smart ones didn't pause to savour this outbreak of quiet: too often it was just the calm at the eye of a tropical storm, violence briefly on hold. They never stopped turning their heads, squinting into the sun, seeking to win a split second to take evasive action from the next attacker.

Those who survived long enough learned to instantly assess the three-dimensional chess game, calculating the odds of killing a pilot lagging from a large formation, or weighing the chances of taking the briefest possible deflection burst at a German before his wingman could retaliate.

According to another Australian pilot on the Western Front, Gordon Taylor, 'Hun' was a word 'used by the British propaganda machine to denote a barbaric type of enemy. In the Royal Flying Corps it simply meant a German aircraft.'

Some decisions, some preparations, had been made long before takeoff. A few stoics, like Little, were willing to dive faster than their peers, their nerve overriding memories of other pilots whose machines had literally let them down under stress. There was a grim jest about a pilot finding himself 'flying in formation with the pieces of his aircraft'.

Some, like Little, practised shooting skills incessantly on the fringes of their aerodrome's farmland, blasting a passing bird, a thrown bottle, a comrade's spinning hat. If you were not born to hunt on the grouse moors of Scotland with a shotgun, raised in the Outback to pot a running rabbit with a .22 rifle, or even learn shooting basics in the Scotch College cadet corps, you had best fast acquire adequate marksmanship in France.

The gifted mastered mid-distance deflection shooting, firing at a patch in the sky ahead of an Albatros or other prey, hoping their spray of .303 Vickers machinegun bullets would coincide with the target.

Little preferred to remove complicated three-dimensional ballistics and aeronautics calculations from the equation. He had the nerve to manoeuvre for point-blank attacks.

He preferred to close to within the length of a cricket pitch, 22 yards, to use a sporting analogy familiar across the Empire in the best-known work of poet, Sir Henry Newbolt. In *Vitae Lampada*, Newbolt suggested that the stoic values of Public School competitive sport—specifically cricket—could be applied to a real battlefield: 'Play up! Play up! And play the game!' was the famous refrain used for propaganda. In this spirit, and given the intense cricket competition between Australia and England, it was hardly surprising, if in dubious taste, that a *Daily Mail* headline writer in 1917 would adopt cricket terminology to exult in Little's downing of three foes on successive days—'Hat Trick for Airman'. War as sport.

Little got so close that he was claimed to have twice struck enemy aircraft in an attempt to bring them down, a risky 20th Century variant of 'coming to blows'. This is one of the Little stories which does not stand up as well as, for instance, his famous 'one against eleven' combat witnessed by ground observers.

But all the guts, skills, and maintenance of nerve across three years of combat would have meant nothing without enduring good fortune. The 20-year-old Little, something of a serial crasher in training, might also have been called 'Lucky Little'.

In a later war, a Melbourne pilot who survived 122 ground attack missions in Typhoons in Normandy and beyond memorably described the fighter pilot's survival chances: 'In the game, it was 10 per cent experience, 90 per cent sheer luck.'

Alec's 21st birthday on July 19 coincided with the Battle of Fromelles, the deadliest 24 hours in Australian history. Australia's blooding on the Western Front was an ill-conceived diversionary attack which saw 5,533 killed, wounded or captured.

Pilots living on the edge of existence needed few excuses for a drink; there are enough reminiscences from his peers about him partying enthusiastically that you can't imagine him not celebrating this rite of passage. Whatever his condition next morning, he did a fighting patrol that day from Dunkirk. In coming days he supported bombing attacks in the Ostend area.

The Australian agony on the Somme resumed on 23 July. The 1st, 2nd and 4th Australian Divisions suffered 23,000 casualties in multiple attacks which seized the rubble heap that had been the former village of Pozieres, before moving a rifle shot away along the ridge to assault Mouquet Farm without success in nine assaults between August 8 and September 3.

Alec Little missed much of the Somme battle. His next foe was pleurisy, an often dangerous inflammation of the lining of the lungs. He was admitted to Haslar, the Navy hospital at Gosport opposite Portsmouth naval base, on August 25. Pleurisy was hardly surprising in a pilot exposed to the bitter cold of high altitudes in an open cockpit. Out of action for almost two months, he was not discharged as fit until October 20.

During his convalescence he married Vera at the Congregational Church in High St., Dover on September 16. Robert Alexander Little, 21 years, bachelor, married Vera Gertrude Field, 22 years, spinster. Alec was staying at the Burlington Hotel, Dover. A photo of the time shows an almost shy-looking uniformed Alec with Vera.

Alec was only a week back from sick leave when he had another close call. The engine of his Curtiss *caught fire owing to too much oil. Landed near Folkestone put fire out.* The same plane put him in hazard the next day as he was returning to Dover. The engine gave out at 100ft and he had nowhere to land. He hit a fence and tore a bottom plane. Any of these multiple incidents might have killed him; you can only marvel at the stoicism and sense of duty that saw most pilots return to the cockpit after near-fatal accidents.

With the Royal Flying Corps under intense pressure on the Somme, the Admiralty created new squadrons to support the offensive. One of these was Naval Squadron No 8, created on 26 October 1916. Its Commanding Officer, Squadron Commander Geoffrey Bromet, was given one flight from each of the RNAS Dunkirk Wings: No 1 squadron contributed six Sopwith Pups, No 4, six Nieuports and No 5, six Sopwith 1½ Strutters. Alec was one of the pilots sent to Naval 8 at Vert Galand aerodrome, former farmland outside Amiens, where Monsieur Bossu's barn provided early shelter.

On November 10 Alec's Sopwith Pup had engine trouble over Thiepval at 17,000ft and he had to return to base. Thiepval was at the heart of the Somme battle; the largest of the British war memorials would be built here.

A fighting partnership was launched on November 14. Little's logbook notes *Sopwith Scout No 5182, Name 'Lady Maud', allotted to me*. He did a patrol in the aircraft which had been repaired after struts had been damaged in combat four days earlier when flown by Alec's friend Edward Grange.

Grange had been quick-thinking. His seniority allowed him to pass *Lady Maud* to Alec, as he recalled in 1970: 'My machine developed trouble: the cowling was badly fitted and allowed a mixture of castor oil and carbon monoxide to blow into the pilot's face. A new machine arrived so I grabbed it and my old machine was allotted to Little, he being younger ... the fume mixture had not troubled my stomach but it was poison to poor Little. Little used to groan at night and his face turned green. When Little reported sick to the Medical Officer—a nice chap but a complete Penguin with no knowledge of the real trouble—the Medical Officer thought it was a case of nerves and was about to send in an adverse report about Little being fit for flying ... thus we nearly lost one of the most wonderful fighting pilots, but fortunately some Sopwith Pups arrived with Le Rhone engines and when Little was allotted a new Pup his trouble stopped.'

Grange survived the war and attended the squadron's 60th anniversary celebrations in October 1976, where he was reunited with the restored *Lady Maud*. Little's widow would later quote a 1970 letter by Grange, who described Little as a 'quick thinking, very likeable character, ready to do more and anxious to get on with it.'

Alec Little's entry in the Australian National University's 17-volume *Australian Dictionary of Biography* was prepared by a Scottish clinical physician from Dumfries, Dr J. C. Little (no relation) in the early 1980s. Dr Little's research included personal communications with Little's CO at Naval Eight, Air Vice Marshal Geoffrey Bromet, Little's friend and fellow pilot Edward Grange, and another pilot, H. Thomson.

'Likeable and friendly with a strong sense of fun, he was a great talker,' was Dr Little's assessment of Alec Little's personality. 'In the air he was a brilliant loner rather than a leader…his armourers calculated that he fired an average of 44 rounds per aerial victory.'

The Sopwith Scout, which pilots insisted on calling the Pup (being smaller than its Sopwith 1½ Strutter predecessor), was the first British single-seat fighter to carry a machinegun synchronised to fire through the propeller. Evolved from Tom Sopwith's 1914 Schneider Trophy-winning Tabloid—and developed with the assistance of Sopwith's legendary Australian test pilot, Harry Hawker—it was tougher than its light structure suggested. It weighed only 500kg loaded. Its Le Rhone nine-cylinder rotary engine could drive it to around 110mph at sea level. Controlling the Le Rhone rotary demanded juggling levers controlling the air supply and petrol flow for all power settings and for changes in height, speed and temperature.

When it came into service at the end of 1916, pilots welcomed its excellent handling. Against the Albatros, a common opponent, its outstanding manoeuvrability compensated for having only a single air-cooled Vickers .303 machinegun against its opponent's twin machineguns. Gordon Taylor, famous postwar as one of Kingsford Smith's co-pilots, wrote in his memoir *Sopwith Scout 7309* of the 'slow popping of my Vickers … compared to the characteristic twin Spandau clatter … like ripping a piece of heavy canvas'.

November 16 was hectic, with offensive patrols at 9.30am, 1.30pm, and 3pm.

One cautionary incident: *A machine began firing at me from under my tail…I hoick* [lifted up sharply] *and turn sharp on the climb and dived beneath it and fired ten rounds when I noticed it was a Spad* [French fighter] *so I broke away.* If your foes didn't kill you, your friends might. Combine the adrenalin and three-dimensional frenzy of air combat; the haze of dawn or dusk, perhaps rain-smeared goggles; fleeting opportunities, and poor aircraft recognition. Deaths from what a later generation called 'friendly fire' were inevitable, even at the modest speeds of Great War aircraft.

November 23 provided a grim example of fire in the air when his tracer set an opponent on fire: *The machine went down at about an angle of 85°. Flames and white smoke were coming out of it all the while. I followed it down to about 6,500ft and saw it still burning on the ground close to a small wood ... [Flt Sub Lt] Hope is missing from our flight.*

This is Alec's first known reference to a missing comrade. Hope would die of wounds in Germany. Alec's first aerial victory, one of four he claimed while piloting *Lady Maud*, was balanced by Hope's loss in the bitter arithmetic of attrition.

We can only guess at Little's reaction to his first victory. Exultation? Relief that it was an enemy machine, not *Lady Maud*, which blazed all the way to the ground? Did he think of the man he killed, or was he able to distance himself from a personal involvement by thinking of downing a machine, not a man, even though he usually fired from point-blank range?

More mechanical problems on November 27:
Comming [sic] *along the Douellens road my petrol pipe got blocked up and I had to land at Bert Angles. I left there at 2.15 & arrived at Vert Galland at 2.20 ... Hope is still missing ... Goble shot down a hun.*

Alec's only known school distinction was for swimming, not spelling. The Allies anglicised hundreds of French and Belgian place names, officially and unofficially: in this case, for 'Bert Angles', read Bertangles. The airfield variously titled Vert Galant/ Galand/Galland is another example. It was on a farm about midway on the road from Doullens to Amiens, and typical of many such airfields. The Mess was an Armstrong hut (canvas stretched over wooden frames bolted together) with an iron stove in the centre. The officers slept in Nissen huts, the ratings in a draughty barn, sometimes sharing it with rats.

On December 3 Alec intercepted an attacking fighter while escorting FE 2bs on a bombing raid. His Vickers machinegun fired only one round: *the H.M.* [hostile machine] *attacked me while I was trying to clear the jamb, my engine was not running very well so I could not climb away, I dived west with the H.M still behind me, It kept up a continuous fire for about 30 seconds. I try to clear the jamb and the H.M.*

again attacked me. To get away from it I was forced to dive more steeply and crossed the lines at 5,000ft. The H.M. was still pursuing me so I dived down and landed in a plough field, the only good field about. I cleared the jamb. He returned to combat, and shot down the first of two fighters: *I opened fire at about 50yds range when it sideslipped and nosedived ... the H.M. was diving plum vertical when I saw him disappear in the mist. I then attacked the second machine.* 'Jamb' was common usage of the time for 'jam'.

His Commanding Officer, Geoffrey Bromet, described this 'busy day' in *Naval Eight,* his history of the squadron as No 8 Squadron RNAS and No 208 squadron RAF: 'After the raid the bombing formation, accompanied by Goble and Little in Sopwith "Pups", did a offensive patrol over the area Mory, Morchies, Velu and Ytres. Never previously had there been so many Huns about and Goble and Little were scrapping all the forenoon. Goble got one down and forced others to land and also broke up several formations. The cold was intense, and to add to Goble's discomfort, he was continually sick ... we heard nothing of Little until long after he was due back, and then he just blew in from nowhere, as was his wont. Apparently while fighting a 'Halberstadt' his gun had jambed and he was forced to land close to our trenches. He managed to clear the jamb, went up again, had another scrap or two, and then, having brought a Bosche down, decided that honour was satisfied, and that he had better find his way home again.'

Some reading between the lines. Little's description of being pursued, with 'continuous fire for about 30 seconds' must have seemed an eternity, even allowing for the distortion of time when in peril. One tracer flicking past would send the adrenalin soaring; multiple bursts, as you tried all the slippery tricks you knew to put off the aim of the man behind, would unnerve all but the coolest pilot. Being 'forced to dive more steeply' would also elevate the heart rate, balancing the hope of escape against the risk of your aircraft losing a wing or two. 'Disappear in the mist' is a reminder that simply seeing a distant enemy was difficult, especially at dawn and dusk, perhaps with smeared windscreen and goggles. It wasn't always the feared 'Hun in the Sun' who made you a statistic, it might be the clever or lucky opponent who dropped from a layer of stratus cloud, or sneaked up from the ground mist. Bromet's reference to Little who 'blew in from nowhere, as was his wont' is early proof of the Australian's enthusiasm for the lone hunt.

Little's doggedness on this day was to be something of a trademark. Many pilots wrestling with a jammed machinegun would have taken the excuse to return to base. He chose to land near the trenches, wrestle with the cocking handle until it extracted the faulty round, and return to the chase.

If there was combat to be had, Little sought it. Call it pluck (a most desired attribute in young men in *Boys Own Weekly*), call it persistence, call it the exhilaration of combat, or bloodthirstiness, even the noble call of Duty. However you interpret it, Little was not one of those to stay within the comforting embrace of the squadron as long as possible, to join battle on cautious terms, to retreat without accusations of cowardice if gun or engine malfunction gave sufficient excuse. Always taking the attack to the enemy, he was a daredevil who fitted the colourful propaganda image of the heroic young men willing to risk all on a daily basis.

A fellow pilot, Flight Commander Robert Compston, described Little in *Naval 8* as 'not so much a leader as a brilliant lone hand. I feel safe in saying that there have been few better shots, either in the services or outside, than this man. I have seen him bring down a crow on the wing with .22 cal. rifle, and break bottles thrown into the air while they were still travelling upwards. What more deadly foe could be found than such a man, armed with two machine guns firing at the rate of 2,000 rounds per minute? Once Little came within range of an enemy he did not give up until, first, the enemy was shot down, his own engine failed, or thirdly, he ran out of ammunition. He had in human guise the fighting tendencies of a bulldog. He never let go.

'Small in stature, with face set grimly, he seemed the epitome of deadliness. Sitting aloft with the eyes of a hawk, he dealt death with unfailing precision. Seldom did he return to the aerodrome reporting an indecisive combat, for as long as petrol and ammunition held out, Little held on until the enemy's machine either broke up or burst into flames.'

The northern European winter was as much a foe as the young men in the Albatros and Pfalz fighters. Some pilots would cover exposed skin with reeking whale oil to deter frostbite. 'Archie', of course, knew no seasons. Little's formation was heavily shelled on a bombing raid over Bapaume on December 11: *My compass was frozen up. At 11am a heavy fog got up and I lost my way. I steered west by a small pocket compass ... my petrol gave out, I landed at Fleury, a small village 4 miles NE of st Pol. I put my machine between two hay stacks for shelter and pegged her down. Next day it was snowing hard so I dismantled the machine with the help of a working party from 60 Squadron.* He is reputed to have entertained his Navy hosts that night with a rendition of Robert Service's Yukon gold rush poem, *The shooting of Dan McGrew.*

Little was escorting bombers again on December 20: *There was a lot of smoke coming from the objective. I saw a hostile machine being chased by a 'pup', the observer was standing up in the machine looking over the tail at the sop.pup. I dived at it and opened fire at about 25 yds range. The observer fell down on the floor of the cockpit. The machine then side slipped and went into a nose dive, I was unable to watch it go far as I was attack by three hostile scout, two type K and one new machine, very fast. I was unable to shake them off my tail so I did a spin and came out at about 10,000ft.*

When I saw the (new German scout) being attacked by two sop. scouts, the other two hostile scouts followed me down. I climbed away from them. My machine was hit in four places.

Later that day he switched to another Pup, as the morning's combat damage to *Queen Maud* was being repaired. *Returned owing to sickness.* More trouble with castor oil fumes?

He had a peaceful build up to Christmas, an afternoon Offensive Patrol on December 24 noted only as *very cloudy, nothing to report.*

There is no logbook entry for Christmas Day, but Boxing Day saw the action pick up amid more bad weather: ... *owing to thick clouds lost my formation near Bapaume. A few minutes later I saw two H.A. type K. I attacked them and they both dived through the clouds after I had fired about 20 rounds at the first one. I then steered a compass course W. and noticed a hostile formation following me. I turned to attack them when three hostile scouts attacked me. I started to climb away still steering west, I saw about 12 H.A. following me. When I reached 15,000ft I saw I was going North by the sun, my compass being stuck. I then steered west by a pocket compass and passed over a very large town. I struck the coast at Calais so went on to Dunkirk for more petrol ... I left at 2.15pm it was starting to rain. I was in a rain cloud all the time flying at a height of 200ft.*

On December 28, Little and his friend Edward Grange were shelled. Little fired at an aircraft shooting at Grange, then:

The other seven hostile machines closed in on us ... I closed in on one scout and came at each other head on. I saw one of my tracers hit and stop on the nose piece of the machine, I also saw a tracer from the enemy pass between my struts. We were so close that I dived to avoid collision ... we passed each other by about 3ft. I saw he had a gun which fired back over the tail, and two which fired through his prop. My engine then stopped and I went westward. It picked up a bit so I came back but it was only doing 1,000 revs.

Fellow pilot Reggie Soar wrote decades later that on the Somme front Little had been 'immediately successful in air combat, as he was with tricks on the ground'. The pilots would often drive into Amiens for dinner at the Godbert, Soar said: 'If stuck behind a car of French officers who would not give way, Little would pull out his revolver and shoot a hole in the rear tyre of their tourer. He never missed. He was an outstanding shot with both revolver and rifle, and was also a collector of wildflowers. He had few equals when it came to air fighting, He would fly the whole length of the British front, from the floods at Nieuport to St Quentin if there was nothing to fight on Naval 8's own Lens–Arras front.'

Little's marksmanship also cost one of his fellow pilots and shooting companions, Ron Sykes, a hole in his RNAS cap as they were searching for targets on the edge of the aerodrome. Sykes threw his cap into the air like a clay pigeon and challenged his flight commander to hit it with his .22 rifle. Little obliged.

Little's Commanding Officer in 1918, the leading Canadian Ace, Ray Collishaw, would recall decades later that by this time

Little's aggressiveness and persistence led his fellow pilots to say 'here is a man who will make his mark'.

'Likeable and friendly with a strong sense of fun, he was a great talker' was a comment in the *Australian Dictionary of Biography* entry on Little.

Somewhere around Christmas, Little wrote to his father outlining his first six months on active service. The letter was printed by the *Scotch Collegian* in 1917:

> Our flight has had a lot to do in the way of fighting, for we are on the part of the line where all the heavy fighting has been going on for the last month or two. I have now got three Hun machines to my name. We have lost two of our pilots in the last fortnight, and I myself was forced to the ground by a fast German Scout yesterday, but got off alright.
>
> I will give you the report, as it is in my logbook, of the two flights in which I got the Huns. To begin with, we fly in formation of five or six machines, just like ships going into action. We have our leader, who carries a flag on his machine.

He gave the logbook entries for November 23 and December 3, summarised earlier: *These two reports will give you a good idea of what we are doing here. Scout No. 5182 is my machine; her name is 'Lady Maud', it was her name before I got her. She is very fast and a good climber. She has brought down four machines, and has been badly knocked about while fighting. After a day's work we are very tired. I have had six months' active service now, and have not been caught. I hope to get through safely.*

At around this time, Little's father would have been bemused to get a letter from a 12-year-old Belgian girl refugee, Mari Madeline De Koninek. On 19 September she wrote from Berek Plage, on the French coast near Le Touquet:

Mr Little,

I have here a very agreeable surprise; meanwhile, I was playing on the seashore, I saw coming in an English aeroplane whom came down very softly on the sand. I was the first with him, and I speak a little English. I spoke to him, and gave him information. It was, Mr, your son, whom, in reward of my little service, gave me his visiting card. It is my duty to tell you, his beloved parents, that Mr, your son, was in excellent health. My daddy, who is a Belgian Commandant, is on the Front, and he is also in good health; and I am very happy too. Mr, my respectful salutations.

The proud father passed it to a Melbourne newspaper for publication.

On 30 December 1916, Alec Little penned a blunt description of the Pup's shortcomings in a report comparing fighting in November and December. The Australian War Memorial passed a copy to Little's descendants:

The enemy has been more daring during the month of December than he was in November.

He flies in formation of about six machines keeping close together and at about 14,000 feet, thus having an advantage over us in Sopwith Scouts who are flying at 12,000ft escorting F.E.2bs.

Two hostile scouts are enough to keep two of our scouts busy while the remaining four hostile scouts attack the F.E2bs.

The enemy dive on us from above and we are unable to return the attack owing to our poor manoeuvring powers compared with the enemy's Type K machine, which can turn quicker than we can, and we are forced to use our superior speed and climb in the defensive rather than the offensive.

We have only one sound method of attack, that is, a surprise attack and our slow firing gun is a great handicap when diving on an enemy or flying below him throttled down.

> When we are escorting F.E s and a hostile formation comes up to attack the F.E. and their escort we are at a great disadvantage, and cannot make any surprise attacks. Whereas last month when we did Patrols alone we were able to deliver surprise attacks on the enemy's scouts and two-seater machines with success.
>
> In the Field
> 30/12/16

His preference for independent, if not necessarily solo action, is obvious in the last paragraph.

As 1916 ended the Allies and the Germans were stunned by the cost of attrition in the battles of Verdun and the Somme, which had ended with hundreds of thousands of casualties. The technological seesaw still tilted firmly towards defence, not offence.

Although the world's first tanks had lumbered at walking pace onto the Somme battlefield, this British invention aimed at breaking the trench stalemate had been more a novelty (and large target) than the effective weapon it would prove later in the war.

The war drove startling advances in aviation as the frail aircraft of 1914 were succeeded by more powerful and more deadly machines. Although raids on Britain by the cumbersome, vulnerable Zeppelin airships had tapered off because of losses to improved defences, Germany's twin-engined Gotha bombers would soon unnerve the citizens of London. A top fighter squadron would have to be withdrawn from the Western Front to reassure nervous noncombatants over the Channel.

The war would always have to be won, or forced into stalemate, by infantry and artillery. The air war would remain a sideshow, even if its drama made compelling viewing from the trenches, and heart-stirring reading from the Home Front.

Military aviation was originally conceived as 'aerial cavalry' (and it adopted cavalry terms, such as 'squadron' and 'scout'). Its greatest contributions were the hard-won images which gave photo interpreters daily detective work in updating fresh trench burrowings, checking changes in rail traffic, and spotting camouflaged ammunition dumps which might indicate a new offensive. Aircraft designed as gun platforms tried to eliminate slower opposing aircraft designed as camera platforms.

Many people thought the true heroes were not the fighter Aces but their prey, those pilots and observers in slow two-seater aircraft, compelled to linger above battlefields, taking photographs or directing artillery fire. For this reason, the British lagged behind the Germans and French in making their Aces front-page news.

Victory scores are notoriously fallible, always to be treated with caution. Criteria varied (the British counted a shared victory as a score for each pilot). Some pilots were obsessive in making the most of their claims; others more relaxed. The criteria for an Ace initially varied, but finally settled on five victories.

Notwithstanding the morale effect of the Gothas (and a handful of four-engined Zeppelin-Staaken strategic bombers, whose wingspan of over 42 metres almost equalled a WWII B-29) bombers had relatively minor strategic impact.

Strafing—ground attack by fighters—was not routine while trench warfare lasted. A pilot driven down within range of ground fire in combat might fire a few bursts into a trench while escaping to his side of the lines. But most pilots willing to pit their skills against another pilot, or endure the random hazards of 'Archie', did not welcome the low-level risks involved in killing a few soldiers. On the other hand, troops suffering regular casualties from artillery fire enjoyed the chance to shoot back at an enemy they could see. Widespread ground attack would not be a common mission until the trench stalemate was broken.

Some pilots' memoirs describe combat almost in the breathless prose of the Boys Own Weekly. One of Britain's greatest Aces, James McCudden VC, buried close to Little after an accident in 1918, wrote in *Flying Fury* about 'our previous little joy-jaunts ... the rascal drove me down to 800 ft ... I went off for some more fun ...

And: 'After a very short burst from the good old Vickers he went down in a spiral dive and crashed also ...

And: 'I was getting a lovely burst into him when both guns stopped ...' I very nearly ran into the tail of the Pfalz at whose pilot I could have thrown a bad egg if I could possibly have got one at that moment ...'

He shot at a Rumpler: 'It dived and after going down 500ft, every one of his four wings fell off and went fluttering down like a lot of waste paper, while the fuselage went down with that wobbling motion which a stick has when one sees it fall.'

An expert on high altitude fighting, McCudden once reached an extreme 21,000ft: 'Both guns stopped, Vickers with broken belt, and the Lewis because of the intense cold.' He suffered agony thawing out as he returned to low altitude.

McCudden loved the Pup: 'I think that one can blame the Sopwith Pup a little for various accidents on other machines because it has got such a large speed variation, is so controllable, and nice, that when a pilot gets on another type he is apt to forget these little things, and at the conclusion it strikes him that flying on the whole is not so easy as the Pup would have one believe. The Pup is so extremely light and well-surfaced that one could almost land it on a tennis court.'

His book concluded: 'I am now in England training the youth, but my heart is in France amongst the gallant boys who are daily dying, and those who are dead, having given themselves to that most wonderful Cause—For King and Country.'

Gordon Taylor wrote in a rather more sobering vein in *Sopwith Scout 7309*: 'Though I deplored the killing and all the other evils of war, for me the actual hunt held in it some irresistible lure ... to stalk secretly and kill was different, cold and desolation, not at all like the fine flush of victory in a duel ...'

The Scout was 'a delightful little aircraft to fly ... as light as a leaf on the wind ... but as an airborne weapon—which is the only purpose of any fighter aeroplane—it was ineffectual, obsolete even before we took it to France (in March 1917, late in its career), critically inferior to the Albatros which had twice the horsepower, twice the armament.' To handle a Sopwith Scout with a thick leather glove was like trying to catch a feather with a cricket bat, he enthused. The little Le Rhones had had to be revved unmercifully. Taylor remembered the burst of blue castrol smoke as each engine started; his full-length leather coat was stained with castor oil.

The death of a friend persuaded him that 'I would have to be alone in the war. There might be passing friends, people around, but the only permanent companion would be Death. Whatever I did, I would do it alone'.

Taylor derided the Press for calling pilots Knights of the Air: 'This embarrassing expression, although the source of many ribald jokes among us, was in fact unusually apt. We were just that, mounted for war upon the little brown fighters with a Vickers gun for a lance.'

Experience and painstaking preparation helped. Taylor practiced spins (to fake being out of control) and 'memorised the pattern of the earth, roads, towns, villages, woods and even the shapes, colours and contours of fields' so he would be completely familiar with the view from the air.

He detested some of the mythology which had built up. 'Unlike the Royal Flying Corps pilots of fiction we were not a disillusioned, lost generation flying with a grog bottle in each pocket and a mirthless smile on our lips. We felt no real hate for the Hun. He was simply the Hun, the opponent, the impersonal enemy. I hunted as a job, and for the thrill of the chase. Hate had no part in it.

'Perhaps I should be able to tell stories of broken, disillusioned pilots drinking desperately in the bar, of emotional outbursts, fear, triumph, hatred, dramatic re-creations in the Mess of the day's fighting. But nothing like that happened. There was drama all right, but it was kept carefully out of our life on the ground. A few of the pilots got tight, mostly individuals who were inclined to get on the grog in almost any circumstances. Some of us were a little edgy, a little over-excited after a show perhaps. But on the whole life on the ground was more or less that of a country club. Sometimes the gaiety at the bar might have been slightly forced ... but never was there any cheap drama.

'There were never any cheap dramatics when people came who returned too often with engine trouble, or who were liable to be sick when there was a difficult escort to be flown. They stayed for a short time, and then they vanished without comment.'

The distant beauty of whirling aircraft ('tiny coloured specks ... a flock of five or six, their colours glinting prettily in the sunlight as they dipped and circled like tiny butterflies in the warm air ... the coloured Albatri of the Hun Circus from Douai') contrasted with killing at short range: 'A black object detached itself from the blazing Rumpler: a grotesque thing with loose and waving ends. The rear gunner had jumped from the death by fire to which my action had condemned him, for the first time I was horror-stricken by the result of war in the air. This now was no triumph. It was a horror from which I wanted to fly away.'

Chapter 8
Apogee: 1917

Apogee: the greatest height reached by a missile, often used in the sense of a pinnacle of achievement

On January 4, Little's first logbook entry for 1917 recorded a bloody introduction to his second year of combat. He opened fire, too late, on three aircraft attacking a British fighter: *the Sopwith Pup twisted to the left and then the left planes came off and it dived to the ground … about 100yds east of the small wood south of Ypres.* Then his aircraft was damaged by heavy A.A. fire near Peronne. *Lieut Todd and Flight Lieut Croft did not return.* Lieutenant A. S. Todd, No 8 Squadron, RNAS, was Manfred von Richthofen's 16th confirmed victory.

Engine trouble plagued him on January 7 during an escort flight. He landed when the engine was missing, resumed his patrol later, but again the engine would not pick up. *I climbed up to 1,000ft and met the De Havilland scouts and patrolled for a while over Warlencourt. My engine was knocking badly so I returned to my base. I had many other small combats. The enemy is firing all tracers. He also came over our lines very often during the forenoon. One De Havilland was shot down. Flight Lieut Grange, Flight Sub. Lawson were both wounded.* Stubborn man, Little, despite a dodgy engine. And what serial violence was involved in the cryptic '*had many other small combats*'?

Losses mounted. On January 23 *FSL Shaw did not return. Last seen over Le Sar … going West.* 'Gone west' was also slang for death. On January 24 Alec made his last recorded offensive patrol in his Sopwith Pup, *Lady Maud: Nothing to report. F. Comdr Mackenzie did not return. Last seen east of Bapaume.*

On February 2 the Naval 8 personnel went to Dunkirk for leave. At Furnes on February 15 they were re-equipped with Sopwith

Triplanes, sometimes nicknamed 'Tripehounds' or 'Tripes'. On March 27 they joined the 1st Brigade RFC, 10 Wing, at Auchel before the Vimy Ridge offensive. By early April, after minor crashes, the pilots had mastered their new craft—and Little would become one of the greatest Triplane Aces.

The brief reign of the Sopwith Triplane would become famous in the annals of the RNAS and the French Navy. It was a formidable machine compared with the Pup, by now outclassed. The triplane's huge wing area gave an unmatched climb rate and great manoeuvrability. The design also offered excellent vision.

Its shortcomings were speed, inability to match some opponents in a dive, and its single machine gun. Nevertheless it had a greater impact on the Western Front air war than its modest production run of around 140 would suggest, before it was superseded in autumn 1917. It partly inspired the Fokker Triplane, the Red Baron's best-known aircraft.

The Triplane's safety in the dive worried many pilots. Another Australian RNAS pilot, Major Bertram Charles ('Bert') Bell DSO DSC, who had commanded No 10 Squadron, recalled this 'serious weakness' in the December 1936 issue of the Returned Services League magazine *Reveille*: 'I lost three or four splendid pilots through their machines breaking up in the air. I was very upset to notice that some of the pilots were naturally beginning to lose confidence in their machines.' One of his flight leaders, Ray Collishaw, volunteered to stage some extreme aerobatics over the airfield ('he did every possible thing he could do to smash that machine in the air') to demonstrate the Triplane's soundness. 'As he taxied back across the aerodrome I could see the slack flying wires and bracing wires shaking violently…a new drift wire overcame the defect.'

Major Bell confirmed another part of the Little legend in a September 1935 article in *Reveille* titled *'Ricki' Little of the RNAS*. He explained how Alec got the nickname from the mongoose in Kipling's *Jungle Tales*. 'I also heard him called 'The Little Butcher' by somebody who did not know him,' Bell added. 'Little's one object was to destroy every German in the sky.' Bell also described Little shooting down three Germans in one action—a colourful yarn not listed in official records. Little's wife and son were not pleased when told of the 'Butcher' reference.

The first of Little's many decorations, a Distinguished Service Cross (DSC), was in the London Gazette on February 16: 'For conspicuous bravery in successfully attacking and bringing down hostile machines on several occasions. On 11th November, 1916, he attacked and brought down a hostile machine in flames. On 12th December, 1916, he attacked a German machine at a range of 50 yards; this machine was brought down in a nose dive. On 20th December, 1916, he dived at a hostile machine, and opened fire at 25 yards range; the Observer was seen to fall down inside the machine, which went down in a spinning nose dive. On 1st January 1917, he attacked an enemy scout, which turned over on its back and came down completely out of control.'

Three days later Little made his first recorded Triplane flight, from the factory at Brooklands to Dunkirk.

Triplane 5455 gave him engine strife on March 11. He burst a tyre landing in a field. Eight exhaust valves had gone. Next day the engine on another Triplane ran poorly, and the pressure pump stuck. He landed at Felixstowe in the dark with no lights put out ... really pushing his luck. Two days later, he'd had enough of Triplane 5355. *Machine not fit to go to France.*

It wasn't all flight testing, ferrying aircraft and no play. He had a starring role in a spirited night off on March 22, recounted by fellow pilot Edward Crundall (later Wing Commander) in his autobiography *Fighter Pilot on the Western Front.* 'In the evening Little, Knight, Cuzner and I went to La Panne and had dinner at the Hotel Terlinck where we drank a lot of wine. The wine affected Little, an Australian, more than anyone else.'

Little chased a dog that had come into the dining room. He followed it under tables, getting some black looks from several Belgians, one a general.

Going home, the pilots took turns carrying Little on their backs for most of the way, barely negotiating a plank over the ditch by his hut.

It's to be hoped he wasn't too hung over. Next morning he made a brief flight in a new aircraft just in from the depot. That afternoon he received a naval signal from Vera: 'Alec arrived 20th March'. They had a son.

On March 26 he delivered Sopwith Triplane N5493 from Dunkirk. He would claim 20 victories in this, his best-known aircraft, a tally second only to Ray Collishaw's Triplane. Written large on both sides of the fuselage, below the cockpit, was BLYMP, his son's nickname. This may have derived from the tubby little RNAS anti-submarine airships, popularly dubbed blimps.

The RNAS permitted some modest personal insignia like this on the basic brown colour scheme. Many German aircraft used bold colour schemes, some with echoes of medieval heraldry; there were also some attempts at camouflage instead of personal identification. The Red Baron's colour scheme was most famous of all. Some squadrons had a theme: at No 10 Squadron RNAS, Collishaw led the 'Black Flight' in his Triplane *Black Maria*; his fellow pilots flew *Black Death, Black Prince, Black Roger* and the more whimsical *Black Sheep*.

Collishaw later regretted the public misunderstanding about the roles of fighter pilots and other fliers. 'The fighter pilot emerged from the First World War as the glamour boy of the conflict and he has since been the subject of innumerable magazine articles, books and motion-pictures,' he wrote in his autobiography *Air Command*. 'Rarely has comparable publicity been given to the many others who flew on artillery observation work, reconnaissance, bombing and a host of other duties.' This was partly because of the technical nature of the work. He mocked post-war writers who turned a few facts about a specific aerial combat into 'pages of colourful material…calling on the imagination to present a complete picture of the exact number of times that each pilot desperately flung his machine into a tight turn, gritted his teeth, snarled at his adversary and cut loose with a lethal stream of lead.' Much of the so-called chivalry of the air war was 'utter nonsense...aerial combat became a completely ruthless business'.

On March 27 the squadron left Furnes for Auchel, just off the main road from Lozinghem and Auchel, west of Bethune and about 12 miles from the lines. 'We were very soon settled comfortably into our new quarters and eager to let the Huns try conclusions with the triplanes,' Bromet wrote in *Naval Eight.*

April 1917 would be forever 'Bloody April' in British air force memory, a slaughter among airman often piloting obsolescent aircraft. While Richthofen and others piled up kills—totalling 150 for the month—the truly momentous news for the month was the declaration of war by the USA on April 6. America's industrial potential, and eventually millions of troops, left little hope for Germany.

Gales and snowstorms hampered operations until April 5, just before the start of the Battle of Arras on April 9. Little saw five German machines on April 5 but had to return with twin troubles—engine failure and a jammed gun.

From *Naval Eight*: 'Little in particular had been making full use of his time since operations started on this Front. Two combats of his deserve special mention as showing his dash and ingenuity. The first concerns a Bosche artillery machine and a gun jamb. One day, whilst on his own near Arras, he saw a two-seater enemy machine doing artillery work. After firing a few rounds at it he had a gun jamb. He tried to clear it and failed, but, instead of going away and leaving the fellow to carry on his work undisturbed, he decided to act as though his gun was O.K., and by constantly diving on the Hun kept the observer firing at him instead of being able to get along with his proper job. His dives and zooms away were so persistent and annoying that the Hun soon tired of the game and cleared off. Having watched him safely away, Little landed at a convenient spot near Arras, cleared his gun jamb, and went up again to look for further trouble.'

Little was about to reach his peak as an aggressive combat pilot. In the 1970s Ray Collishaw wrote a character study of Little for Keith Isaacs' book *Military Aircraft of Australia 1909–1918*. 'Here between Ypres and Arras he accomplished his phenomenal victory score, and by autumn Little was pre-eminent as the "Cock of the Walk"'.

April 7 saw one of Alec's most famous combats, usually listed as against pilots of the Richthofen Circus. One perspective was from an anti-aircraft artillery unit of the 3rd Army, gunners practised in precise observation:

> At 6.45p.m. on 7/4/17, a Sopwith Triplane, working alone, attacked eleven hostile machines, almost all 'Albatross' scouts, N.E. of Arras. He completely out-classed the whole patrol of hostile machines, diving through them and climbing above them. One 'Albatross' scout, painted red, which had been particularly noted by this Section, dived on to him and passed him. The Sopwith dived on him and then easily climbed again above the whole patrol, drawing them all the time towards the Anti-Aircraft guns. As soon as they were in range, the Anti-Aircraft guns opened fire on the patrol, which turned eastward, and the Sopwith returned safely. The Officers who witnessed the combat report that he manoeuvring of the Sopwith triplane completely out-classed that of the 'Albatross' Scout.

In another comment on this fleeting, frantic epic, Edward Crundall quoted Commanding Officer Geoffrey Bromet's report on air combats from April 6–19: 'Pilot was then attacked by about 11 similar scouts from above whom he managed to outmanouver and climb away. This combat was confirmed by Sergt Dempsey, No 25 Squadron RFC.'

Little's logbook entries for the date are less than enlightening. At 10.05am he flew an Offensive Patrol at 16,000ft for 1hr 20min ... *Nothing to Report.* His second [un-timed] entry is for a 1hr 20min Offensive Patrol at 8,000ft. In full:

When near Arras at 7,000ft I observed two machines about same height as myself being fired on by A.A. I proceeded to attack one of the machine(s) which was coloured a bright red with blue wings. I noticed tracers passing between the planes & he dived away. At the same time I was attacked from the beam by a machine of similar type but coloured green. I outmanoeuvred him & drove him down in a steep spiral firing at him all the time when from a height of 2,000ft I saw him fly into the ground near the trenches NE of Arras. I was then attacked from above and my machine was hit in several places including the oil tank. I climbed away to 10,000ft and returned home.

As there are no significant combat reports in his logbook for days either side of that incident, it seemingly has to refer to the same event. In which case he chose not to go into any detail about an 11-to-one clash. Why not? Might it sound like 'shooting a line'? It also makes you wonder what other incidents never made his logbook during his three years of combat.

If the anti-aircraft gunners read the combat sequence correctly—that Little attacked the 11 Germans, rather than the other way around, or a clash at random—it confirms his audacity and eagerness to tackle large formations on his own. Some sources speculate that the all-red Albatros might have been the Red Baron. David Hammond's painting of this one-sided encounter hung in the Australian War Memorial for years.

Whatever the details of this mismatched combat, word of the Triplanes' agility spread, and some British pilots believed the Germans were avoiding them. For instance, the New Zealand Ace, Captain Forster Herbert Martin Maynard, wrote post-war that the sight of an easily identifiable Triplane was enough to send an enemy aircraft home. The moral effect of this new type was considerable at that time.

Interviewed decades after the war by Douglas Whetton for the WWI aviation journal *Cross & Cockade (USA)*, Little's former wingman Reggie Soar offered some colourful reminiscences of Little:

> I remember Little very well, he did some unusual things on the Somme. He was a stubby little Aussie and an expert shot. Little never paid much attention to orders such as this; just before the Battle of Arras, he was out early, returning only late for dinner, and having to apologise for being late before he sat down next to me. He whispered that he had shot down five enemy aircraft, and he had a beautiful smile of 'go and tell me I'm a bloody liar.' I told him that he would be court-martialled if he had been near the lines. But this didn't seem to worry him too much.
>
> The next morning the CO read to us a signal he had received from the Canadian General commanding the section Lens-Arras. He first called out Little, and then began to read a most glowing account of how a triplane called 'Blimp' had attacked eight Albatros DIII's getting five down in the trenches, and would we call and collect them as they were littering up the place, or words to that effect.'
>
> (This may have been a spectacularly inflated report of Little's combat against 11 aircraft on April 7, the only pre-Arras combat listed in his logbook.)

You could bet it would be eventful if you flew with Little, Soar went on:

> Flying together at 1500ft near Savy, we saw a small fire near a wood. Little, a curious laddie, went down on top of it to see what it was all about. He soon knew, it was an ammunition dump which went off with a terrific crash. I saw him rise up almost to my level with a suddenness beyond belief. It was the funniest thing.

Little was a great pilot with a triplane and there was no catching him once he dived. *He would pass you, wing tips moving towards each other and even the centre section moving* [my italics] and by the time you were down to his level his Hun would be piled up in the forward trenches.

For Little, April 11 was a quiet day, no flying recorded; for the unfortunate 4th Division Diggers thrown into the hastily-planned battle at Bullecourt to support the Arras offensive, it was a disaster. The two brigades involved had 3,300 casualties, and more were captured—1,170—than in any other Great War engagement.

Little saw 14 enemy aircraft on a patrol on April 15, but *could not get within range.* He sounds disappointed at not being able to tackle 14 aircraft.

Bad weather all day on April 17 meant an opportunity for another party, Crundall wrote: 'A few of us were invited to dinner at 25 Squadron RFC, where there was a rough-house before we left. Both Squadron Commander Bromet and Major Cherry joined us in the scrimmages, and the partition between the Mess room and the sitting room was charged down.'

Little abruptly cut short a test flight in Triplane 5467 on April 20 after just five minutes: *Unsatisfactory. Right main top spar bent.* Pilots needed no reminder of the fragility of their aircraft. Later that day Alec helped a visiting pilot, Ira ('Taffy') Jones, whose aircraft had a new engine fitted. Jones recalled in his book *Tiger Squadron* that 'Collishaw has been a trump ... one of his flight commanders—Little by name and stature—was also very kind to me. He is a celebrated Hun-strafer and has a pocketful of decorations already. How many he'll have when the war ends, God only knows.' Jones survived the war with 37 victories, and served as a Wing Commander in WWII.

Next day Little nearly flew into a British aircraft being attacked by three German fighters (one blue, one white and a brown one). His gun jammed. He followed the gliding British plane until it flew into the ground near Douvious Wood: *I landed to see if I could be of any help. The engine & controls were shot about but the pilot & observer were alright.*

He fought an outstanding German during a patrol on April 23: *the H.A. manoeuvred very fast and the pilot was an exceptionally brilliant one, he looped and side rolled most of the time and I was only able to get my sights on him twice and then for a very short time. I fired about 80 to 100 rounds at him and we beat him down from 10,000ft to 6,000ft when he went into a cloud and crossed his lines and got away.*

'Beware of the Hun in the Sun' was one of the combat mantras drummed into inexperienced pilots. Later that day Alec spotted an enemy over Thelus at 16,000ft: *He was unable to see me as I was in the sun ... I fired and saw tracers hit his fuselage and the observer stopped firing. The machine went into a spin for about 10,000ft and then flattened out again. I dived on it but could not catch it up.*

On April 24 there was an element of farce, as well as comradeship among aviators, when he was sent up to attack a German approaching the airfield: *I dived and attacked ... I noticed the observer was not returning the fire so I closed in on him ... I observed my tracers going into his fuselage at a range of 10 to 15 yds. He then nosedived and I dived after him. He landed in a field and I was unable to get my engine (going) after the dive and had to land alongside the H.A. I ran into a ditch and turned over. I got out of my machine & went over to the Germans and took them prisoners. The pilot told me he knew he would never get back when he saw me coming to attack him. His name was Lieut Neumuller, & Observer-Lieut Huppetz.*

Naval Eight's author reported: 'This fight had an amusing finish. Forced down owing to loss of petrol (Little had hit the petrol tank) the enemy machine landed without damage in a field near Les Facons. A few seconds later Little followed, and, in his haste, made a rough landing and turned upside down ... when Little crawled out of his machine to claim his prisoner, the German pilot saluted smartly and said in English: "It looks as if I have brought you down, not you me, doesn't it."... during the fight the observer had got himself hopelessly entangled in his machine gun belt ... and it took Little and Neumuller quite a time to free him. Neumuller said he thought the war ought to be over during the summer because England was starving. He was very surprised when at lunch at No 1 Balloon Wing Headquarters a large plate of meat was put in front of him.'

Fellow pilot Edward Crundall reported that 'the three of them went to lunch and soon they were the best of pals, exchanging souvenirs and relating their various experiences. The Germans spoke good English and both had been awarded Iron Crosses.' (There would be a touching postwar sequel for Vera Little.)

Alec notched up another forced landing when his engine failed on April 28.

On April 29 he was in combat beside another Melbourne pilot serving in the RNAS, the redoubtable Richard Minifie. Most of Minifie's 21 kills were as a teenager. He was one of few pilots to win three DSCs.

Little and Minifie both attacked a formation of five Albatros scouts: *When over Douai aerodrome one of the Albatros scouts which both I and Minifie were firing at went down in a spin and I saw him crash on the aerodrome itself.*

Little had to play some tricks on April 30 when pounced on by the proverbial Hun in the Sun:

> *A red Albatros scout with a larger engine than the rest dived on me from out of the sun. My gun jambed and I tried to break off the engagement but the H.A. kept pace with me and open(ed) fire on me, shooting away my pump and hitting the planes, so I then stopped and stunted. I then got under the H.A. and stopped there. I turned when it turned and dived when it dived. The H.A. could not find me. I got the jamb clear and fired on the H.A. which was about 20ft in front of me and about 10ft above me. Half the fuselage and an engine was all I could see through my sight. I saw tracers hit it. It started to climb then stalled and went down in a dive turning slowly. I last saw him at 1,000ft when I lost him in the mist. I saw two more scouts to the East of me and went to attack but then found I had no ammunition left (my machine was hit in three places during the combat).*

His opponent may have been flying one of the first 180hp Albatros D5s, introduced in April 1917.

A near-collision and another fortunate escape on May 2 as eight Albatros scouts attacked a formation of DH4s: *I dived on the nearest Hostile scout when I was fired at from behind by another. I turned sharply and got under his tail and fired about fifty rounds at a range of about 10–15yds. The H.A. came so near that I had to take my eyes off the sight to avoid colliding with it. The H.A. turned over on its side and then nose dived. I was not able to watch it as my engine stopped at this moment. I glided west and was attacked by four hostile scouts. I dived towards our lines & when over them spun down, I got my engine going again when at 300ft.*

Alec was promoted to Flight Lieutenant on May 7. Two days later there was a rare reference to a strategic retreat: *I was very much outnumbered, I landed at St Eloi to obtain reinforcements.*

On May 12 he failed to clear a jammed Vickers machinegun despite taking it to pieces in the air—not advisable when you could be jumped at any moment.

Four days later the squadron moved to Mont St Eloi airfield, nearer the front lines, almost in sight of Vimy Ridge, recently captured from the Germans. All ranks were under canvas, with the aircraft in Bessoneau hangars.

A brief duel on May 18: *the observer fired about 20 rounds at me and then fell over the gun.* Late afternoon on the next day, *To Dunkerque for Decoration*, the only logbook mention of medals (his Distinguished Service Cross).

Little didn't mind trailing his coat behind the German lines. On May 20, he returned from duty at Dunkirk via Nieuport, then south about one mile behind the German trenches at 10,000 ft. He fired at one aircraft. Next day he topped all his many forced landing stories, managing to return to the British lines when his engine was hit by machinegun ground fire. Landing safely near Nine Elms, he borrowed a horse and rode to St Eloi. Imagine colleagues' relief, and teasing, when he arrived back late on horseback. 'Aerial cavalry' at last!

Combat discretion was sometime exercised. After a fight on May 20, Little and Flight Commander Booker (an Englishman who had spent three years at school in Melbourne) *were then attacked by a large number of scouts so we retired west.*

There was an incident-packed late afternoon flight of 1hr 20 minutes on May 23. Little and FSL Knight attacked three two-seaters: Knight's gun jammed and he returned home. Little was attacked by four Albatros; he hit one, they left. He crossed back into Allied lines, climbed to 17,000 ft, recrossed the lines and attacked a scout, which dived away. He then attacked three scouts, which went east. They returned, he dived again on them but was attacked by eight more scouts: *my engine stopped. I glided west for a while but was forced to dive away from the scouts. They overtook me so I went into a spin & spun down to 1,000ft & crossed our lines. My engine began to go very badly but I managed to get back to St Eloi.*

By May 1917, the pilots had the opportunity to go on to light duties, or take leave, from a new aerodrome on requisitioned farmland on a flat, elevated grassy plateau above the Walmer Castle estate on the Kent coast, south of Deal.

In May 1917 a German seaplane had torpedoed a British ship off the Downs anchorage. To protect shipping from similar attacks, the RNAS established Walmer aerodrome above Walmer Castle, a coastal artillery fort built by Henry VIII as one of his defences to keep the Spaniards at bay.

Walmer served two purposes, according to the *East Kent Mercury* report in 1920 on the dedication of the Walmer Aerodrome Memorial to fallen RNAS pilots who had served there. The report refers to combat stresses rarely mentioned in wartime.

'The aerodrome here was luckily found without any trouble, but the difficulty was to find pilots,' Air Commodore Charles Laverock Lambe told the guests at the dedication. 'At the time we were very hardly pressed to find sufficient pilots in France, and all pilots out there were working very hard—far harder than one would have wished if there had been more pilots available. But a flight had to be found for Walmer, and we seized the opportunity to select six of perhaps the best but most highly strained and over-wrought pilots, who had served in France for many months, and we brought them back to Walmer where they served the double purpose of attempting to protect the shipping in the Downs and at the same time having the opportunity to enjoy a complete rest from active service conditions in France.

'Now the majority of the pilots who were working with the RNAS in those days in France—nearly 75 per cent—came from overseas. They were very largely Canadians, but they also came from South Africa, Australia, New Zealand, and in fact every Colony and Dominion there is.

'The difficulty was to rest these pilots, who were very gallant fighters, and always keen, but had no homes to go to. If they were sent on leave for a well-earned rest, they had nowhere to go but London, where they had to stay at a hotel in default of somewhere else, and they came back with no rest at all, and with their nerves worse than when they left France ... the success of sending these pilots back to Walmer of course depended entirely upon whether they got the rest at Walmer which we hoped they would get. Thanks to the hospitality which was offered by everyone in the vicinity, the aerodrome immediately fulfilled its purpose ... they all wanted to come to Walmer. When they got here they did not want to go on leave, so that in a short time the original six was extended, until we were able, by the co-operation of the Admiral at Dover, to bring back a complete squadron ... and give them two months' rest at Walmer.

'These overseas boys from Canada and other Dominions, when they came to Walmer, experienced for the first time in their lives probably some idea of home life in England—the only experience of home life which they had had from the time they left their own countries ...

'The squadrons, and especially the pilots, went back to France from the rest at Walmer as absolutely different people. They were enabled to do far more work. They came back keen, and they were able to do far more flying, and for more time; and during the strenuous days in the middle of 1918 it was only through the rest they had had during the previous winter that many of these squadrons could have existed. *The strain on the pilots was enormous* (my italics), and we were not getting enough to keep it up. Every pilot, I am convinced, looked back on his time at Walmer with pleasure.'

Alec was granted 14 days' leave. Vera and baby Alec waited just across the Channel. Alec returned from Dover to Dunkirk on June 9.

Edward Crundall wrote of dining with Little when the Australian was stationed at Dover, living with Vera and young Alec on Marine Parade. 'Husband and wife chaffed each other a great deal and she tried to be as tough as he was. He told her she would be scared stiff in an aeroplane and she replied that he could not frighten her. 'Right', he said, 'I will take you up.'

Highly illegal, but what adrenalin-fuelled fighter pilot liable to 'Go West' any day would worry about piddling disciplinary consequences?

Alec arranged to land in a field to pick Vera up in a Sopwith two-seater, with Crundall following in a Triplane as they flew to the Isle of Sheppey and along the coast to Margate. 'I think Mrs Little must have said something to her husband to indicate she had proved her point that he could not frighten her, because, as we approached the field, he did every manner of stunt. He looped, rolled, spun and all sorts of things and then, instead of the field, he landed at Walmer aerodrome. I landed just in time to see Little carry his wife to a car. She was in rather a bad way so he drove her to the local hospital.'

Back in France, Little enjoyed extreme good fortune on 13 June when the flight of four Triplanes attacked seven Albatros Scouts over Douai aerodrome. He sparred with a plain black Albatros for about ten minutes until his controls jammed. He side-slipped down to 7,000ft with two enemy after him. He managed to free the controls, and attacked the two pursuers *who thereupon went east. They were both badly hit and my machine was hit seven times.*

He received a bar to his Distinguished Service Cross (DSC) on June 22. The *London Gazette* noted: 'For exceptional daring and skill in aerial fighting on many occasions, of which the following are examples:

> On 28th April, 1917, he destroyed an Aviatik, on the 29th April, he shot down a hostile scout, which crashed. On the 30th April, with three other machines, he went up after hostile machines and saw a big fight going on between fighter escorts and hostile aircraft. Flt Lieut Little attacked one at 50 yards range, and brought it down out of control. A few minutes later he attacked a red scout with a larger machine than the rest. This machine was handled with great skill, but by clever manoeuvring Flt. Lieut. Little got into a good position and shot it down out of control.'

On 23 June the London *Daily Mail* published the latest honours list, accompanied by a story on Little headed *Air Hat-Trick*, with a secondary heading *A German Down Each Day/For Three Days*: 'A feature of the honours announced today is the bar to Flight-Lieutenant Little's DSC, for bringing down a German plane each day for three days.' It quotes the citation.

The somewhat frivolous 'air hat-trick' heading is hardly surprising, given the growing rivalry in cricket between England and Australia.

When *The Herald* of Melbourne reproduced the *Daily Mail* story on 8 September, it was followed by a purported 'interview' with Little which seems more fiction than fact, an outrageous 'beat-up'. Whether Little decided to pull the journalist's leg, or the journalist decided not to let accuracy stand in the way of a chauvinistic morale-booster, the result is laughable, if you forget the growing Rolls of Honour on both sides. A selection:

> 'The Huns,' says Lieutenant Little, 'claim to have mastery of the air, and you see a lot in our papers on that subject, but the Hun never comes very far from his aerodrome, which is about 15 miles on his side of the lines. Of course, they come

out and fight in great numbers sometimes. Once I met 11 and I was alone. They tried to cross our lines, so I attacked the last man and shot him down, the others fired a few shots at me. One shot went through my oil tank, and my machine ran out of oil. I turned and faced the 10 of them and they went for their lines. If there had been 20 they might have fought me. I then glided back home.'

If that absurdity reeked of *Boys Own Weekly*, the sneering chauvinism reached new depths as the writer retold the amusing incident on April 24 when Little had forced down Lieutenants Neumuller and Huppetz, and later took them to lunch: 'When he saw me he knew it was up, and put his nose up to climb, but my machine could climb just about four times as fast as he could, so I soon caught him again. His observer could not fire at me, he was so frightened. The Germans are afraid of the type I fly, as it is about three times as fast as their fastest scout. I have red streamers on each side of my machine, and he had heard of me before out meeting … one of the Huns could speak English and said he knew he could never get back home when he saw me attack him, so he landed before he was killed.'

Little's 'quote' concluded: 'So you see the Germans don't have it all their own way in the air. They come over our side about once a day, and we patrol over their aerodromes all day long. They won't come and fight, but sneak about and pounce on a spotting machine, down it by about 10 to 1, and then run home as soon as they see one of our scouts coming.' If a copy of this 'story' ever reached the squadron, you can imagine Little having to shout the bar, to chants of 'you can't believe anything you read in the papers'.

A rather more confronting incident came near his aerodrome on 26 June when Little engaged a two-seater flown by pilot Gefreiter Ernst Bittoff, with Lieutenant Paul Schweizer as observer: *I attacked it head on from a little below. I then did a roll which brought me out about 20 yds behind going in the same direction as H.A. I then stalled up and fired a burst of 20 rounds at a range of 50 feet, the H.A. then stalled and dived west. I dived after the H.A. which dived past the vertical and & came back east on its back. Something then fell out. I think it was a man. The machine glided round on its back & I caught up to it again. I saw a man crawling along the fuselage, trying to get on the bottom (the machine was still on its back and was now on fire.) I close (d) in on the H.A. and fired about 20 rounds at it & the man fell ... the machine carried on down to about 100 feet when it broke up & crashed near Achiville.*

His combat report made soon after landing was more direct, describing how he saw the second man crawling along the fuselage *so I fired at him and he fell off.*

How might you interpret this? The aircraft and its frantic crewman were doomed. Was this the *coup de grâce* (literally, 'blow of mercy') to end a fellow aviator's suffering? Or did he kill in cold blood (or hot blood) to ensure that his victory was confirmed?

Interviewed more than half a century later, Little's wingman that day, Reggie Soar, added another element to the situation. He was quoted in *Cross & Cockade*: 'Something fell out ... the German was then flying upside down going back towards the German lines. This was annoying to Little who wanted it down on our side of the lines. We then saw the observer frantically trying to get on the bottom of the aircraft, then the top of the bus. Heaven knows what for, we had no parachutes in those days. Quite deliberately Little closed in and at point blank range shot him off and he came tumbling down arms swinging and screaming his head off. I can see Little's grin as he landed, and remember him saying to me that I should have seen the gunner kicking like hell trying to get right way up. Little, along with Mannock who landed almost daily at our mess, was the only man who really hated the Germans.'

If this recollection was accurate, might Little's remark have been black humour instead of a callous comment? Pilots often laughed in the face of the death they risked with each flight. One of the British pilots' most popular drinking songs—often belted out to the tune of *My Bonnie Lies Over the Ocean* as they relieved tensions in the Mess—told of 'a poor aviator' who lay dying in his aircraft wreckage, urging his mechanics to ...

Take the manifold out of my larynx
And the cylinders out of my brain,
Take the piston rods out of my kidneys,
And assemble the engine again.

Some pilots (rarely the British) had macabre insignia; funeral icons, a coffin, skull and crossbones and more.

Ray Collishaw had a cynical jest to describe layers of protection for an observation aircraft. The best four pilots would circle the slow-moving twin-seater at close range. If four less-skilled pilots were available, they would be sent 500ft higher as the 'sacrifice flight' where the diving Germans would probably strike first. Should the squadron be at almost full strength, the inexperienced newcomers and other expendables would be 500ft higher yet as the 'super sacrifice flight'.

Black humour or not, the episode reminds us that millions of young men raised on the Sixth Commandment were given a temporary exemption to kill; this was a 'just war' for all sides. In the fury of combat, fiercely-held individual beliefs or military rules of engagement were often forgotten or discarded.

On 29 June, Little and Reggie Soar attacked seven aircraft over Lens. Little saw his tracer hit the rearmost enemy; it turned left, and Soar fired on it. Soar reminisced years later: 'Little got behind me, but I wasn't having that, he had a bigger name than me and I wanted to see how he would behave in this predicament. Little was now leading me but made no effort to attack until he suddenly saw the last man had got a little lower and aft of his formation and he very neatly dived below, yanked up, fired no more than six rounds and down went the Hun. I think it was a bit ambitious just the same; we were only two. I dived on another and the remaining Huns dived on me, too many to do any harm as they were in one another's way; and it was all over and clear sky in less than two minutes. That's the kind of thing you get into being with Little, and so it went on.'

Alec pulled another 'stunt' on July 5 after shooting down a DFW north of Izel. On his way home, he saw another DFW about to attack a balloon. He attacked but his gun jammed and was only able to fire single shots. *I managed to keep the DFW away from the Balloon by stunting around it.* Not a bluff you would want to try regularly.

At St Eloi, in July, the squadron began to switch from the Triplanes to Sopwith Camels, named for the humped fairing over their twin Vickers guns. On July 6 Little refers for the first time to flying a Sopwith Camel; it had engine trouble. The Camel was the most famous and most successful of all British fighters of the Great War, with 1,294 victories credited to Camel pilots. Leonard Rochford liked the Camel very much: 'It was a complete contrast to the Pup which was docile and stable with its 80hp Le Rhone engine and dihedral on both top and bottom planes. The Camel had a 150hp Bentley rotary engine and dihedral on only the bottom plane; it was an unstable machine and the powerful engine gave it a vicious kick to the right as soon as it was airborne, which had to be corrected by using a lot of left rudder. However, no aeroplane could be manoeuvred so quickly and that was its great advantage in combat.'

More luck for Little on July 7 when he was shelled by Allied anti-aircraft batteries and had to give up pursuit of a German aircraft. Friendly fire again.

During action on July 12 he saw the Canadian RFC Ace, Capt Billy Bishop, shoot down a German near Vitry: *Capt. Bishop & myself then attacked another E.A. & during the fight the German pilot waved a white handkerchief or something* (traditional gesture of surrender) *so I stopped firing at it, but seeing that he turned East* (homewards) *I opened fire on him. I think he was wounded. He dived down and went away very low.* Chivalry at last—if briefly? Billy Bishop VC would survive the war, with 72 victories.

A familiar problem on July 13: '*Both my guns then jambed & I broke off the engagement.* Faulty .303 ammunition often jammed the Vickers machineguns. Pilots had to interrupt their ceaseless search of the sky, trying various techniques to clear stoppages, wrestling with the cocking handle to try and clear a jam. Some really professional pilots checked hundreds of rounds and loaded their own machinegun belts, hoping to detect oversize rounds which might otherwise cause their deaths.

Late on July 7, Alec *saw some night flying machines & attacked them but it was too dark to see much.*

He was promoted to Flight Commander on July 18. There was no flying the next day, and Edward Crundall describes sundry relaxations: 'Johnson is flying a model aeroplane, which he built, and it goes quite a long way. Little made a submarine out of a piece of wood, to which he fitted metal fins. It is propelled by elastic and he is demonstrating it in the swimming pool (dug by the pilots, with a wooden framework to which balloon fabric was attached to make it waterproof).There are long intervals with nothing to do. This can become very boring …

'In the evening a supply of champagne was obtained…the piano was played, songs were sung, and it developed into a merry evening. Quite a number had rather too much to drink and it affected them in various ways. Little was running around with the squadron dog, Titch, which went under the floorboards after a rat, and Little followed it there …

'Jenner-Parsons had crouched in a corner of the room. Suddenly a wild expression came into his eyes and he saw Thornley sitting on the window ledge peacefully smoking his pipe. He jumped into the air, dashed across the room, and butted Thornley through the open window. After that the party got really rough and one after the other were thrown into the swimming pool.' Away from the roughhouse outlets of tension, Little also made model aircraft.

Next day Alec chased a DFW over Lens: *Before I had time to engage it the E.A. put its nose down and spun, the tail plane then seemed to crumple up and the machine crashed.*

Many pilots feared the fragility of their own aircraft as much as the threat of an enemy. When Gordon Taylor first flew his Pup, he was concerned over criticisms of the aircraft's strength. He coolly did a loop to stress his aircraft, so he could be fully confident of the little fighter in combat. Both parties survived the loop. 'I felt a great wave of triumph, of release, of confidence in my aeroplane…I sang at the top of my voice and shouted in the open air where now there was an infinite, delicious freedom. I wanted to kill this bogey (so I) looped her six times over the hangars.'

Many pilots flew their aircraft cautiously, saving wild manoeuvres for desperate situations. Little, on the other hand, had a name for out-diving his colleagues in attack. Reggie Soar borrowed Little's triplane while Little was on leave, and found he was overshooting on attacks, coming in too fast. He later discovered that Little had moved his seat forward so that he could dive faster— 'the crazy clown!'

Little's preferred close-quarter combat also risked collision in a whirling dogfight. Keith Isaacs wrote in *Military Aircraft of Australia 1909–1918* that Little collided with the tailplane of an Albatros, and had to land with a cracked undercarriage, and also deliberately ran his wheels over the top wing of a DFW in an attempt to force it down. There are no known logbook references to these incidents.

While some of the pilots might have been men of iron, their aircraft were certainly not. The exception, and a sign of the revolution the war brought to aviation, was the first all-metal aircraft to go into series production. Hugo Junker's J1 observation and ground attack aircraft of 1918 was a hint of things to come.

On 19 July, Little received France's *Croix de Guerre.*

Getting within range of ground fire was risky. The Red Baron, who warned his pilots of that danger, is widely regarded as having been killed by Australian ground fire in April 1918. On July 22, Little drove an Aviatik down to 500ft near Douvray. *I was being fired on by machines from the ground … I observed a machine in a hole in the ground and fired both guns. I saw tracers hitting the hole and the gun stopped firing.*

On July 27 Alec fired at a machine gun from a height of 50ft, silencing it; next day he attacked a German machine (gun) in Crumpet Trench, killing four of the crew and putting the gun out of action. *The Germans fired at me with rifles & a great many machine guns, but only hit my machine once.*

His logbooks after this date have been lost.

During July he shot down 14 aircraft.

On 31 July, as Little prepared for a rest spell in England, the British in Flanders launched the Third Battle of Ypres, best known, and loathed, as Passchendaele. The drive to reach the German submarine bases on the Belgian coast was literally bogged down as agricultural drainage systems shattered by shellfire could not cope with protracted rain. Scenes of this nightmarish waterscape, captured by the Australian official photographer Captain Frank Hurley, are among the best-known images of Australians at war.

British and Dominion casualties approached a third of a million men. Australian forces suffered 38,000 casualties over eight weeks in combat at Menin Road, Polygon Wood, Broodseinde, Poelcapelle and the First Battle of Passchendaele. The village of Passchendaele was eventually captured and the dreaded Ypres Salient was widened by a few kilometres.

On 1 August 1917, Little's Commanding Officer, Geoffrey Bromet, wrote his official report on Little's service under his command 'on board No 8 Squadron, RNAS' from 26 October 1916 to 1 August 1917: 'He conducted himself to my entire satisfaction. A most loyal, keen and & capable young Officer with few, if any, equals as a Fighting Pilot. He has brought down a total of 32 German machines, 28 of which have been accounted for since April 4th 1917. For conspicuous bravery, great initiative and skill on numerous occasions on the Somme, & Lens & Arras Fronts he has been awarded the D.S.O. & D.S.C. & Bar.'

On August 5, Little was posted to Walmer for a rest. By then he had destroyed 37 aircraft.

Little kept a letter from Brigadier General Gordon Shephard DSO MC, who controlled Naval 8 and other squadrons. Shephard wrote on 2 August 1917: 'I am sorry you were spirited away in such a hurry, as I did not get the opportunity of telling you how much your gallant work and example have been appreciated. I expect the German Aviators will rejoice if they hear you have left this front.

'Well I hope to see you back again some day and that your deeds will be still further rewarded.' Shephard, a flying officer from June 1913, died in a flying accident in January 1918.

Little's decorations spread across his medal bar. He was made a companion of the Distinguished Service Order (DSO) on August 11: 'For gallantry in action and for exceptional skill and daring in aerial combats. Since the 9th May, 1917, besides having driven off numerous artillery aeroplanes and damaged six hostile machines, he has destroyed six others. On the 26th June, 1917, an Aviatik being seen from the aerodrome he went up to attack it. He engaged it and fired a burst at close range, and the enemy machine stalled and went down in flames.'

A bar to the DSO followed on September 14:

> For exceptional gallantry and skill in aerial fighting. On 16th July, 1917, he observed two Aviatiks flying low over the lines. He dived at the nearest one, firing a long burst at very close range. The enemy dived straight away, and Flt. Lieut. Little followed him closely down to 500ft, the enemy machine falling out of control.'

> On 20th July, 1917, he attacked a D.F.W. After a short fight the enemy machine dived vertically. The tail plane seemed to crumple up, and it was completely wrecked.

> On 22nd July, 1917, he attacked a D.F.W. Aviatik and brought it down completely out of control. On 27th July, 1917, in company with another pilot, he attacked an Aviatik. After each had fired about 20 rounds, the enemy machine began to spin downwards. Flt. Lieut. Little got close to it, and observed both the occupants lying back in the cockpits, as if dead. The machine fell behind the enemy's lines and was wrecked.

> Flt. Lieut. Little has shown remarkable courage and boldness in attacking enemy machines.

In October he was posted to Guston aerodrome on top of the cliffs above Dover. On December 11 he was Mentioned in Despatches.

If officialdom had recognised Little's deeds with a raft of medals, how did his comrades regard him?

Geoffrey Bromet wrote in *Naval Eight* that judged from the standpoint of actual flying, 'Little was just an average sort of pilot with tremendous bravery and a flair for finding his way about. There was nothing particularly accurate or finished about his flying, but for getting the last ounce of an aeroplane as an offensive weapon, he had few equals.

'Air fighting seemed to him to be just a gloriously exhilarating sport, and he had been doing regular work over the lines for many months before I can remember him showing any sign of fatigue or nervous strain. When out on a job of work he never ceased to look for trouble, and very little escaped those keen eyes of his. In combat, his dashing methods, close range fire and deadly aim made him a formidable opponent, and he was the most chivalrous of warriors.

'As a man, he was a most lovable character, and a sportsman in the truest sense of the word. When not flying his greatest joy was to go out after rabbits or rats with other sportsmen ...'

Evan Hadingham's *The Fighting Triplanes* quotes another Naval Eight pilot, Herbert Thompson: 'Little was the clumsiest lander and in the air drove his triplane to the verge of disintegration. He had an eye like a telescope. I remember one patrol when we were flying at 17,000ft and he picked out a well-camouflaged two-seater crawling along at 1,000 feet. He waggled his wings and was away in a tremendous dive. None of us could keep up and he had got the German into a spin (pilot probably killed) with a burst of fire before we could arrive. What the speeds of our dives were I shudder to think. And in the same week, Dixon, spinning his triplane with engine on at 10,000 feet, tore all his wings off.' On Little's fight against 11 enemies, Thompson asked: 'What better testimony to a man who had such a wonderful flair for air fighting?'

Hadingham quotes Australian-born Flt Cdr George Goodman Simpson on Little: 'A most brilliant air fighter, probably one of the finest shots in France. He is reputed to have used an average of seven bullets for every plane he shot down. At any rate it was his boast that he had wrecked as many British planes on landing as he had brought down Germans in the air. That was probably a gross exaggeration but he was certainly very careless in landing any machine. I wouldn't say he was clumsy for when he wanted to fly well he was a very brilliant pilot.'

During 1917 the squadron had moved from St Pol to Vert Gallant [sic] (1 February), Bertangles (28 February), Marieux (26 March), Furnes (1 June), Bray Dunes near Dunkirk (6 September) and Walmer (1 November).

Little totalled his flying time as Dunkirk 19hr.25min; Somme 50hr 10 min; Furnes 9hr 20; Auchel 78hr 25.

Now he was able to spend much of winter with Vera and Alec at 'Beachcroft', 5 Droveway Gardens, St Margaret's, near Dover. This deadly shot joined shooting parties on the Walmer Castle estate.

His son Alec would write in the 1930s of his mother having witnessed German aircraft attacking Dover. An RNAS car picked up Little from 'Beachcroft', with his boots, collar and tie still in his hand. Young Alec was told of his father attacking 13 aircraft: 'My father's gun jammed and he had to rely on his wit ... he came spinning through the midst of them ... the Germans were so bewildered that they turned out to sea, with my father following.' Quite a bedside story. He gave a very fine performance of his stunt flying in August 1917 in the presence of Earl and Countess Beauchamp and senior officers, his son added.

On December 1, Alec made his will, with Vera as executor. The timing of the will seems somewhat belated. The witnesses were RNAS pilots, Flight Sub Lieutenants Alfred Lawson and George Simpson, who went on to score eight victories.

A truculent Colonial? Alec Little, 20, seemingly glares at the photographer taking his portrait by a Caudron GIII for his pilot's licence, issued on 27 October 1915. In early 1916 senior officers' complaints about Little's attitude threatened his dismissal from the Royal Naval Air Service. (Courtesy: Imperial War Museums Q69148)

THE SCOTCH COLLEGIAN

Edited by Boys of the School.   Published at the end of each Term.

Above Age of Innocence: Alec Little (left) and his younger brother James at Scotch College, Melbourne, 1907. Alec left school in 1912 to work as a commercial traveller for his father, an importer of medical texts.

Below Masthead of *The Scotch Collegian*.

Flight Commander Alec Little and his wife Vera, a Dover girl.
(AWM AO5196)

Vera Little. (AWM 5201)

Wistful pilot: Robert Alexander (Alec) Little of the Royal Naval Air Service.

1958

LITTLE, Robert Alexander
    113, Punt Road, Windsor, Victoria, Austra-
                                        lia.

Born 19th July 1895   at Hawthorn, Victoria,
                                        Australia
Nationality British
Rank or Profession
Certificate taken on L. & P. Biplane
At London & Provincial School, Hendon
Date 27th October 1915.

Little's pilot licence of 1915.

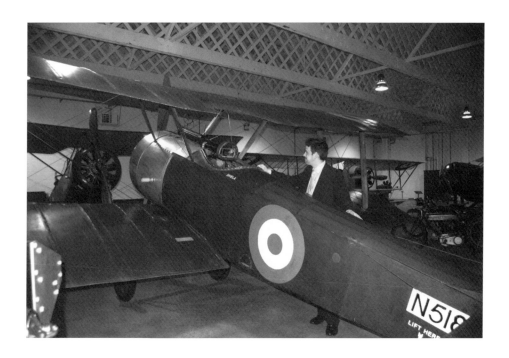

Remarkable survivor: At the Royal Air Force Museum on the site of London's first airport at Hendon, education officer Vernon Creek stands by the Sopwith Pup ('Lady Maud') in which Alec Little claimed his first four victories in 1916. The adjacent 'Aussie' Pups information panel celebrates 'formidable air fighters such as Captain R.A.Little' who flew the Pup—but does not identify this as Little's aircraft. Little learned to fly at Hendon.

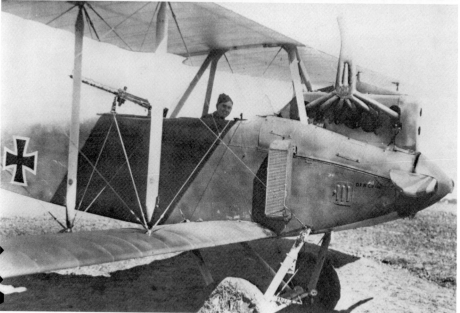

Above Victor: The only known photo of Little's Sopwith Triplane bearing his son's nickname, Blymp.

Below Victim: two of Little's more fortunate opponents were forced down in this DFW observation aircraft on 24 April 1917. They survived and were entertained in the squadron Mess; the pilot, Lieut Friedrich Neumuller, wrote to Little's widow after the war, praising a 'very honourable and noble' adversary, launching a Christmas correspondence that lasted for years. (AWM 5408)

Army Form W. 3348

Combats in the Air. · 25

CR 158/18.

Squadron : No.203 Squadron RAF.

Type and No. of Aeroplane : Sop. Camel, D3416.

Armament : 2 Vickers syn Guns.

Pilot : Flt Comdr R.A. Little.

Observer : None.

Date : 22/5/18.

Time : 11-40 approx.

Locality : Near ST LEGER.

Duty : Off. Patrol.

Height : 10,000 ft. 3

Result
{ Destroyed ......Yes.......................
{ Driven down out of control .=.........
{ Driven down...........................=

Remarks on Hostile Aircraft :—Type, armament, speed, etc.

Albatross 2-seater.

Narrative.

Whilst flight were attacking a Kite Balloon I had to retire owing to pressure failure.
I met a two-seater Albatross Scout which I attacked at close range. EA dived and crashed into a railway cutting near ST LEGER and was completely wrecked. I was at 1000 ft and observed no one get out of machines.

[signature]

FLight Commander.

Aeroplane destroyed.

[signature]

Commanding Officer.
No.203 Squadron RAF.

Alec Little's combat report after bringing down a two-seater Albatros near St Leger on 22 May 1918. He was killed in action five days later.

Opposite & above Alec Little, aged by war.

(AWM AO 5200; Fleet Air Arm Museum, Nowra)

Predator: Reginald 'Reggie' Soar, who often flew with Little, photographed in 1916.

(Courtesy Fleet Air Arm Museum, UK)

Above Informal memorial: pilots of 203 Squadron RAF at Little's grave at Wavans cemetery. The squadron mechanics crafted the Celtic grave cross. Little's widow brought it to Australia when the formal cemetery was built. In 1978 family members donated it to the Australian War Memorial, where it has long been prominently displayed with his medals. Little's Commanding Officer, Major Raymond Collishaw, a famous Canadian fighter pilot, is second from right.

Below The Celtic Cross crafted by the squadron mechanics for Alec Little's grave in Wavans Cemetery. He died aged 22, not the 23 shown. (AWM AO5195)

Above Formal memorial: six stained glass windows dominate Scotch College's Memorial Hall built to honour more than 200 former students killed in the Great War.

Below Little's widow passed this plaque of Little's medals to their son. Scratched on the back is 'Given/to my/Blymp/from Mumsie/1918'. It is in the Australian War Memorial.

(AWM Rel/04031.007)

Above To earth: Daniel Melin, mayor of the small village of Noeux (left distance) quizzed old villagers without being able to pinpoint Little's crash site in 1918.

Below An Australian visitor laid this Scotch College pennant on the grave of a notable Old Boy, Alec Little.

Little's widow and son (foreground) laid a wreath at the dedication of the RNAS Memorial at Walmer aerodrome in Kent in 1920.

Visitors to the Australian War Memorial look at Little's medals and temporary grave marker in 2008.

Left Portrait of Vera Little postwar.

Right The hero's son, also Alec, grew up to head the electronics workshop at the Physics Laboratory at Melbourne University.

DEATH AND GLORY

NOTED AUSTRALIAN AIRMAN MEETS THE FATE OF A HERO

CAPTAIN R. A. LITTLE KILLED

Deep regret will be felt by his personal friends, and a sense of loss by every Australian who admires heroism, at the news of the death in action of Flight Commander Robert Alexander Little, conveyed by private cable message to his father, Mr James Little, of "Ryde", Punt road, Windsor. Flight Commander Little was married, and his wife and young son have made arrangements to return from England to Australia at once.

The record of Flight Commander Little was probably unequalled even in the glorious annals of the Royal Flying Corps. His exploits accounted for at

IN HONOUR'S CAUSE

FLIGHT-COMMANDER R.A. LITTLE

least 76 German airmen, in addition to the occupants of other enemy machines, the destruction of which was not officially confirmed. The record of this young Victorian of 22 rivalled that of the greatest known fliers, and his decorations included the D.S.O. and Bar, the Distinguished Service Cross with two Bars, and the Croix de Guerre. He was attached to the Royal Naval Air Service, and before the end came had had many amazing escapes from death. He was recently in London after an extraordinary adventure, in which, flying at a height of 15,000ft., he attacked six enemies. His machine was

peppered, and spun down to 10,000 feet, where he was attacked by a second flight of six enemies. The controls of his machine were completely destroyed, the tail was shot off, and the petrol tank fell out, hitting his pilot on the head. His plane hurtled down out of control, flattened out at 300ft., and crashed down in No Man's Land, where soldiers came to the rescue. His only injury was a scratched nose, while his aeroplane was reduced to matchwood. He refused the command of a squadron because it would involve the cessation of his fighting. He was keenly anxious to add to the list of his victims.

Flight-Commander Little was educated at Scotch College. On July 27, 1915, when he was 19 years of age, his father sent him to England to attend an aviation school. It cost him £500 to qualify and he was then appointed to the Royal Flying Corps, subsequently being attached to the Royal Naval Air Service.

In February, 1917, he began his long and glorious record by winning the Distinguished Service Cross. On May 12 of the same year, when he had the defeat of 13 enemy machines to his credit, he was awarded the first Bar to the Cross, and also won the Croix de Guerre. On July 1, 1917, when he had established the record of having destroyed 23 enemy machines, he was awarded the Distinguished Service Order. Since then he had won a second Bar to his Distinguished Service Cross and a Bar to his Distinguished Service Order.

His brother, Private James S. Little, fought with the 14th Battalion on Gallipoli, where he took part in the battle of Lone Pine. He subsequently returned to Melbourne.

Flight Commander Little used many types of aeroplanes in his exploits, his favourite Scout having being christened the "Lady Maud." Before he acquired this machine it had already brought down four enemy planes.

On one occasion, when Little was flying alone, he met 11 German machines, which tried to cross the British lines. He attacked the last man, shooting him down. The others fired a few shots at him. One shot penetrated his oil tank, and his machine ran out of fuel. He turned about, put his 10 enemies to flight, and glided back home.

He had numerous single combats, in one of which he drove down a German plane and took prisoner the two officers on board, both of whom had Iron Crosses. He performed numerous daring feats while engaged in bombing raids, and on one occasion saw four German planes attacking a British machine. He drove off the enemy aircraft, and subsequently destroyed one of them.

The deepest sympathy is felt for his relatives in their loss. But Australia will remember the young airman who came forward unafraid in the hour of peril, scorning, as he said himself, to live the life of "an old coward." Fate answered his unspoken prayer, "Put me, I pray thee, in the forefront of the battle." And now he is no more – but before he perished he wrote his name in the sky, and he died on the wings of fame.

'One against Eleven' captures the frenzy of Alec Little's most famous combat, fighting alone against 11 German scouts northeast of Arras on 7 April 1917. British artillery observers reported how the manoeuvring Sopwith Triplane 'completely outclassed' the Albatros scouts, possibly from the Richthofen Circus.

(Painting by Max Ordinall reproduced with permission of the Royal Australian Navy)

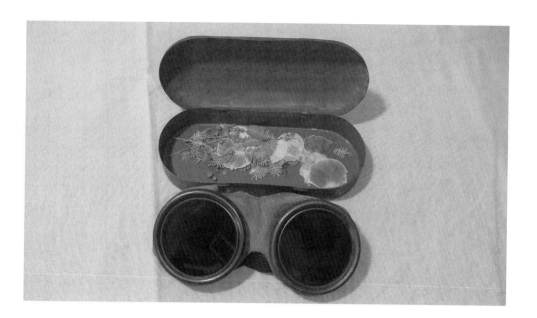

Above Alec Little's goggles and case, with dried wattle and pansies, were among a trove of Alec Little's belongings found several years ago at a waste transfer station in Queensland, Australia. See *Elegy from a country tip*, page 123.

Below Penny with impact mark, and possible bullet fragments.

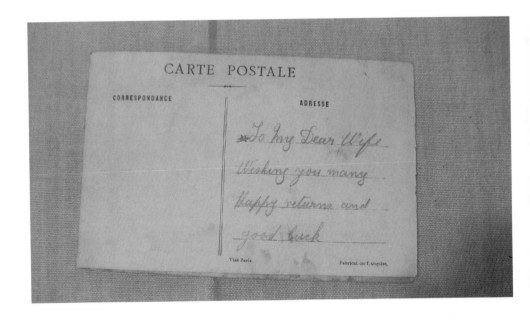

Above Photograph of Alec Little's son, found folded over this gold sovereign, stitched in the front flap of Little's helmet.

Below Note on French postcard.

(Courtesy: Royal Australian Navy Fleet Air Arm Museum)

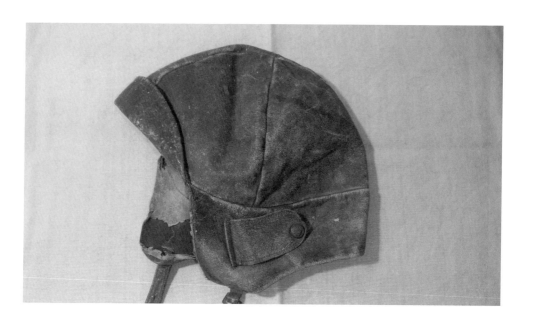

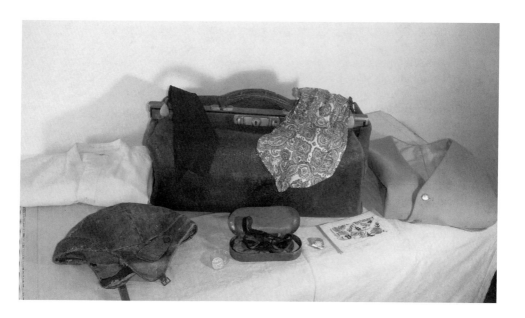

Above Little's flying helmet. A photograph of his son Alec folded around a gold sovereign was found stitched inside the front flap.

Below Alec Little possessions found inside the Gladstone bag (rear) include (foreground, from left) helmet, gold sovereign, goggles, baby photograph and embroidered silk 'Happy Birthday' handkerchief. Rear, from left, silk shirt, tie, cravat and waistcoat.

(Courtesy: Royal Australian Navy Fleet Air Arm Museum)

Above Terry Hetherington, manager and senior curator of the RAN Fleet Air Arm Museum at Nowra (NSW), with Alec Little's helmet, and the tattered photo of his son Alec Jr and a gold sovereign, found stitched inside the helmet. The aircraft is a replica of Alec Little's Sopwith Pup of 1916.

Below Helmet, goggles, baby photograph and sovereign.

Chapter 9
Eclipse, 1918

As the winter of 1917/1918 eased, the Germans planned their last throw on the Western Front. Their situation was desperate. While the Russian Revolution had allowed them to transfer troops from the Eastern Front, hundreds of thousands of Americans were pouring into France, backed by massive American production.

On 17 March, the Melbourne pilot Dick Minifie, acting CO of 1 Naval Squadron, came down behind the German lines. He spent the rest of the war in 'a relatively comfortable prisoner of war camp', as he later told his family.

On March 21 the Germans successfully launched the *Michael* offensive with the greatest bombardment the war had seen, and new infiltration tactics. Open warfare was back and the RNAS pilots were soon in action trying to stem the tide of soldiers in field grey pursuing the retreating British and their allies. This triggered a far greater call for ground attack.

Little had been appointed a Flight Commander on 1 January 1918. The squadron left Walmer for Bray Dunes, near Dunkirk, the next day. In March he is reported to have declined a desk job; his descendants say he requested a transfer from Dover to RNAS 3 Squadron commanded by Raymond Collishaw. Collishaw later wrote that Little's spirit remained in France, and that he yearned to be back in action.

By now the Confidential Reports made comments like 'exceptional courage and gallantry … Flight Leader of great daring … Brilliant fighting officer … Good command of men'.

By almost any assessment, Little had an outstanding character, according to Collishaw: 'Bold, aggressive and courageous, yet he was gentle and kindly. His hobbies were shooting rats and gathering wild flowers. He studied botany and he grew a wildflower garden by his quarters.'

A Collishaw tale of Little attempting to hypnotise his pilots before dangerous missions to give them extra courage and determination was challenged by Leonard Rochford: 'Difficult to believe and, as I knew all these pilots well, I can definitely say none ever mentioned to me that this took place.' Rochford recalled some occasions in the Mess when Little pretended to hypnotise a pilot as a joke. He spoke also of Little's love of nature and remarkable eyesight and powers of observation. On a country walk, the eyes that were often first to spot a faraway aircraft could pick out animal trails that others had missed.

Collishaw reckoned pilots in other flights were grateful not to be under Little's command: 'They thought he was far too inclined to seek and to take far too many unnecessary risks.' Collishaw said Little didn't adopt the usual practice of gradually introducing a new pilot to combat: 'He believed that a man was born with, or without, courage. He would take a new pilot very low over the Lines to 'blood' him, whereupon all hell would break loose.' Pilots who stuck with Little received further training; those who failed would be passed over.

Little's rise to fame was a long arduous struggle of dangerous adventure, Collishaw added. 'Each morning the prospect of seeing another day seemed dim. He grew to believe that his destiny was divinely protected.'

On 1 March the squadron moved to Mont St Eloi; on March 28 to Treizennes; on April 9 to Liettres (Estree Blanche); on May 15 to Filescamps Farm.

While his 1918 logbook has vanished, the combat reports in the squadron history record his last months, involving claims for 11 aircraft. Although the UK National Archives discovered in 1989 that a Public Records Office reader had removed some WWI and WWII aviation documents, many were recovered, and the thief was convicted. Many of Little's original signed combat reports from

1918 are still in the files and may be viewed under rather more stringent security arrangements than before.

Years of Army/Navy rivalry over aviation eased on April 1, 1918 when the Royal Air Force was created by amalgamation of the Royal Flying Corps and the Royal Naval Air Service. Little transferred to the RAF as Lieutenant (Temporary Captain) Aeroplanes and Seaplanes. He marked the occasion with *a fight with 10 Fokker Triplanes which dived on us from above. We dived west until over our lines, when I came round a cloud and engaged the last man of the formation. After about 200 rounds were fired the machine did a steep dive and the lower port plane came off. The machine fell through the clouds about 3 miles west of Oppy.*

On April 7, now with 'No 203 Squadron RAF', Little's flight *was dived on by 10 Triplanes ... I dived on three E.A. which were attacking Merlyn and fired at an Albatros scout from 50 yards. After about 20 rounds from each gun the EA turned and went down out of control through the clouds. After the fight was over I returned to look for the E.A. and saw a machine crashed about one mile SW of Violaines.*

The confusion of the German advance is typified by an incident with his former squadron at La Gorgue on April 10, when the Portuguese front collapsed. In thick fog, the Camels were grounded, and the aerodrome and locality were under attack. Bromet's successor, Major Christopher Draper, had the Camels pushed into the centre of the airfield and burned to prevent their capture. The squadron was re-equipped with 20 aircraft within two days.

Writing in *Cross and Cockade* in 1978, Douglas Whetton said three of Little's contemporaries, Aubrey Ellwood, Yvone Kirkpatrick and Ronald Sykes, all recalled Little's hostility to the Germans. He quoted Sykes: 'Little himself appeared to have a complete disregard for danger.' Sykes told how Little had his flight 'stooge around' within range of an anti-aircraft battery, while Little pretended to be hit, stunting to ground level and then attacking the gunners. Whetton quotes a letter from Kirkpatrick to his parents: 'By the way Little is an awful nut in the RNAS. He's brought down 44 Huns, and has the luck of old Nick himself.'

On April 11, an Albatros paid the price for lagging behind its fellows: *I fired a burst into it and it turned over and spun slowly down ... I followed it down to 2,000ft and watched it crash about Neuve Eglise.*

The RAF communiqué No 1 for April 15 noted that 'Capt R. A. Little, No 203 squadron, attacked an E.A. 2-seater from 200 yards closing to 20 yards range, firing all the way. The E.A. observer was seen lying in the cockpit and the enemy machine dived into the clouds...on it coming out Capt Little attacked it again, firing from about 20 yards. The E.A. stalled and went down emitting smoke, and was seen by other members of the patrol to fall in flames.'

The cult of the Ace still did not sit easily with the British. For instance, as late as 24 September 1918, 'Wireless Press No 9 issued by HQ RAF' opened with 'Only rarely are brilliant records of British Airmen made known ... it is now announced that Major Raymond Collishaw ... has destroyed 51 machines. He is described as a 'brilliant squadron leader of exceptional daring.'

April 21 should have been Little's last flight, but somehow, improbably, he survived. He had attacked the last Pfalz scout of a formation of 12, and watched it fall for about 10,000ft over Vieux Berquin, completely out of control. *I was then attacked by six other E.A. which drove me down through the formation below me. I spun but had my controls shot away and my machine dived. At 100ft from the ground it flattened out with a jerk, breaking the fuselage just behind my seat. I undid the belt and when the machine struck the ground I was thrown clear. The E.A. still fired at me while I was on the ground. I fired my revolver at one which came down to about 30 ft. They were driven off by rifle and machine gun fire from our troops.* Little's blood must have been up—perhaps it was partly because he had fallen into a manure heap, as fellow pilot Ronald Sykes reported later. Whatever the cause, he recklessly exposed himself to fire his revolver at the German aircraft. It was the first time Little had been shot down.

Richthofen was killed on this day. Although Little had fought with aircraft from Richthofen's 'Flying Circus', there is no record of them having fought each other.

By now the German offensive had stalled.

On 18 May, Little and Flt Lt Hayne fired at a Pfalz scout which was seen to go down out of control.

On 22 May, retiring with pressure failure, Little attacked a two-seater Albatross scout and sent it crashing into a railway cutting near St Leger. *I was at 1,000ft and observed no one get out of machine.* On the same day he brought down a DFW near Morchies. He rounded off a busy day with a flight at 8.10pm, chasing a Fokker Triplane which passed over the aerodrome. Overtaking it at Estaires, he fired a burst and the aircraft turned over and went down out of control, disappearing into the mist.

***

In Raymond Collishaw's absence, Alec was acting as Squadron Leader.

It was a critical stage in the war. His family would see the war news in the Melbourne papers—'At Height of German Swing to Paris'—'Germans Capture Soissons', 'Australia's Fighting Army; Divisions Seriously Weakened.'

Germany's Gotha bombers were a nightly irritant along the front. Little and Collishaw had previously flown in moonlight periods, fruitlessly seeking the intruders. Night flying a single-seat fighter with only basic instruments was hazardous, especially in poor weather.

While bad weather has killed thousands of pilots and passengers, it wasn't an issue on the evening of 27 May 1918. A high pressure system west of Ireland maintained fine and settled conditions across much of southern England and northern France. It brought clear skies, a light wind from the northeast and evening temperatures around 12°C. And it was only two days past full moon—not what the Europeans called Hunter's Moon (that usually came in October, a month after Harvest Moon), but well suited to the consummate predator Alec Little.

Little's friend Rochford recalled that not long after darkness fell, pilots drinking in the Mess at Ezil Le Hamel heard a bomber overhead. Little left the Mess. Soon afterwards the drinkers heard the sound of his Bentley rotary engine as he took off with full throttle into the night.

'Later 'Kiwi' Beamish came into the Mess and confirmed that Little had gone up in his Camel to pursue the bombers—not for the first time,' Rochford remembered.

Given fine weather and a bright moon, a search was possible. In the immensity of the night sky Alec would look for clues from antiaircraft fire, perhaps a searchlight, perhaps distant bombing. With great good luck he might see a fleeting twin-engine shape against the sky or moon, or the red glow from a Gotha's engine exhausts. But the young Australian's run of astounding good fortune was about to end.

As the hours passed, the tension grew as his colleagues realised that, at best, his fuel must have been exhausted. One way or another, he must have returned to earth.

Not until next morning did Major Booker of 201 squadron report that he had identified Little's body in his crashed Camel.

Little was not to see the victory so many had died for, nor know of the Diggers' vital role in helping to stem the last German ground attacks near Villers Bretonneux.

'Robert Alexander Little, one of the bravest men I have known, loved air fighting and was quite without fear,' Rochford concluded.

Collishaw returned from leave next day. 'Nothing could be learned beyond the fact that Little's aircraft had crashed after he had been fatally wounded in the groin,' he wrote later. He dismissed speculation that a Gotha rear gunner might have fired the fatal shot: searches of German records had been fruitless. 'The great Little fell to a random bullet fired by an unknown assailant. Little's fighting career was an inspiration to his contemporaries and his example was a tribute to the high standards of Australian manhood.'

In *Golden Eagles*, Peter Firkins' book on Australian fighter Aces, he quotes a 1968 letter from Vera Little: 'It was early morning before Alex was found, and by that time it was too late. It was obvious that the matron of the hospital, from whom I heard later, wished to spare my feelings in the matter, but I realised that even if Alex had been found soon after he crashed his wounds would have prevented his recovery.

'His position as acting CO of 203 Squadron should have prevented his flying, but like so many young men of his generation, duty came first, and even his father's letter to "take care, and do nothing rash" had no effect. Courage was his most commendable virtue, for he believed on this depended all the others. Although it is over half a century ago, I can recall him as vividly as if it were yesterday, and this had made up for all the lonely years between.' Little's skull and an ankle had been fractured in the crash.

Little was buried at Wavans British Cemetery, 14 kilometres northwest of Douellens and 32 kilometres northeast of Abbeville. This was a 'hospital' cemetery; serving 21 Casualty Clearing Station, based at Wavans between 18 May and 18 September 1918. Casualty Clearing Stations had to frequently relocate ahead of the German advance.

There is no indication in the War Graves Commission records that Little was first buried at Noeux, as suggested in some accounts. With padres often attached to Casualty Clearing Stations, it's possible Little had a few words said over his shrouded body.

Otto Wolter, a German buried at Wavans, almost certainly died while being treated at the Casualty Clearing Station. It was not unusual: there are 5,790 identified Germans in Commonwealth War Graves Commission cemeteries in France and 1,631 in Belgian cemeteries.

The Commission maintains well over a million war graves as well as memorials honouring the 750,000 war dead with no known grave. It honours casualties equally without distinction of rank, race or creed. Cemeteries with over 40 graves display the Cross of Sacrifice representing the faith of the majority, a simple cross embedded with a bronze sword.

***

Melbourne's papers eulogised Alec Little. Most prominent was *The Herald*, with a triple-deck heading on 31 May:

DEATH AND GLORY
Noted Australian Airman Meets the Fate of a Hero
Captain R. A. Little killed

Deep regret will be felt by his personal friends, and a sense of loss by every Australian who admired heroism and daring, with the news of the death in action of Flight Commander Robert Alexander Little …

The record of Flight Commander Little was probably unequalled even in the glorious annals of the Royal Flying Corps. His exploits accounted for at least 76 German airmen, in addition to the occupants of other enemy machines, the destruction of which was not officially confirmed … the record of this young Victorian of 22 rivalled that of the greatest known fliers … before the end came he had many amazing escapes from death.

The writer concluded 'Australia will remember the young man who came forward unafraid in the hour of peril, scorning, as he said himself, to live the life of "an old coward". Fate answered his unspoken prayer, "Put me, I pray thee, in the forefront of the battle" and now he is no more—but before he perished he wrote his name in the sky, and he died on the wings of fame.'

His portrait was captioned 'In Honour's Cause'.

The Scotch Collegian of August 1918 noted in Little's obituary that

his record is probably unequalled even in the glorious annals of the Royal Flying Corps. His exploits accounted for at least 76 German airmen, in addition to the occupants of other enemy machines, the destruction of which was not officially confirmed.

...before the end he had many amazing escapes from death. He was recently in London after an extraordinary adventure, in which, flying at a height of 15,000ft, he attacked six enemies. His machine was peppered, and spun down to 10,000 ft, where he was attacked by a second flight of six enemies. The controls of his machine were completely destroyed, the tail was shot off, and the petrol tank fell off, hitting the pilot on the head. His plane hurtled down out of control, flattened out at 300ft., and crashed down in No Man's Land, where soldiers came to his rescue. His only injury was a scratched nose, while his aeroplane was reduced to matchwood. (This sounds like a version of the April 21 combat where, after crashing, he fired his revolver at aircraft shooting at him.)

He refused the command of a squadron, because it would involve the cessation of his fighting. He was keenly anxious to add to the list of his victims.

***

Little's friend, Major Roderic ('Stan') Dallas, survived Little by only five days, dying in a clash with three German triplanes on 1 June. The Queenslander was a personal friend, Vera Little said years later: 'At Guston aerodrome at Dover he would come to our cabin for tea, and took great pleasure in amusing our baby son.' Dallas was second only to Little on the list of Australian Aces, with 39 official victories. His grave at Pernes war cemetery bears the inscription *Not Lost But Gone Before.*

Charles Booker, who had identified Little's body, almost survived the war. On 13 August 1918 he died trying to protect his inexperienced wingman from a group of Fokker DVIIs. He had 29 victories. Edward Crundall wrote in his diary of Booker, his shy flight commander: 'He says he hopes the war will go on forever because he loves air fighting, and if the war were to end he is afraid he might not be able to find a suitable job.'

The former Victorian railwayman, Stan Goble CBE, DSO, DSC was asked postwar to serve as an adviser on the formation of the Australian air force. In 1924 Goble and Flying Officer Ivor McIntyre made the first successful flight around Australia. Goble retired from the Royal Australian Air Force in 1946 with the rank of Air Vice Marshal, after a career marked by inter-service rivalries and epic personality clashes with other senior officers.

Major Bertram ('Bert') Bell DSO, DSC, returned to the family's pastoral properties near Boonah in Queensland. From destruction, he would turn to creation, winning awards for farming innovations. He was distressed at not being accepted for service in WWII.

Richard Minifie saw out the war in a prisoner of war camp, and returned to Victoria in 1919. He quit university studies to join the family flour company, later serving as president of the Federal Council of Flour Millowners of Australia. During WWII he served as a Squadron Leader in the Air Training Corps.

Few people, even his family, knew the war record of the modest, courteous Minifie. One of his daughters, Prue, remembers a rare occasion where he spoke of deeply regretting the number of young pilots 'sent out with only a few hours of flight training, with no chance of coming back … it made me feel like a murderer.'

Chapter 10
Remembrance

From an Australian population of fewer than five million, 416,809 enlisted. More than 60,000 were killed and 156,000 were wounded or taken prisoner.

The numbing losses prompted a wave of memorialisation that reached into the smallest community, changing the cultural landscape forever. Communities paid for thousands of war memorials destined to be the focus of Anzac Day and sometimes Remembrance Day services. The statue of a slouch-hatted soldier, often posed head down resting on rifle reversed in the form of military commemoration rather than in some more militaristic gesture, was a ubiquitous and prominent symbol of loss.

Later generations might not recall some of the names on the memorials—Bullecourt, Pozieres, Mesopotamia, Flanders and their deadly company—but even the least history-minded passer-by would sometimes skim the names, perhaps with several victims from the one family, and wonder what might have been.

There were layers of passion here beyond community recognition of those who had served, or made The Supreme Sacrifice. The propagandists seeking to support the volunteers abroad had tried hard to shame others into uniform. Sometimes this was faintly ridiculous, like recruiting posters with the bestial Hun about to bayonet Australian women and children cowering at the base of a familiar Australian farm water tank. Less appealing—to those who believed in Australians' sense of fair play—was the public or anonymous offering of a white feather, implying cowardice, to a young man not in uniform. This small-minded sign of the times seemed particularly shabby when an anonymous donor demonstrated the same lack of courage imputed to the recipient.

The sensitivity to those who served, and those who did not, is sometimes pointed. In the small Queensland village of Montville, in the range behind Noosa, the local Great War memorial is two marble panels on the front gateposts of Montville Hall. There are six names under Fallen; 33 under Enlistments; and six under a rather startling heading, Rejected—presumably those would-be volunteers who failed the medical. That emphatic statement of volunteerism hints at the wide community divisions between the representatives of those who chose to volunteer, and those who waited on conscription. Some communities had long memories for those perceived as shirking their duty; some who sought high office post-war risked abuse, or oblivion, if they could be painted as having evaded war service. The bitterness of the wartime Conscription debates also exposed sectarian bigotries now almost vanished from national discourse.

Beneath the thousands of statues on the memorials, familiar patriotic phrases (The Fallen, or Our Glorious Dead) headed the long lists of the dead.

Families perhaps found some consolation in writing inscriptions—usually patriotic, religious or family remembrances—to those kin who had a headstone amid the numbing geometry of hundreds of war cemeteries. Thousands of the unidentified lay under headstones typically engraved 'A Soldier Known To God'. To honour these lost legions, some nations exhumed Unknown Soldiers for interment in national shrines. On 11 November 1920, a soldier representing all the young men of the British Empire killed during the Great War was entombed in Westminster Abbey in London, and an unknown French soldier was buried under the Arc de Triomphe. Other nations followed.

Australians debated a similar commemoration in the 1920s, but did not follow through until the 75th anniversary of the end of the Great War. The body of an unknown Australian soldier recovered from Adelaide Cemetery near Villers-Bretonneux in France was interred in the Australian War Memorial's Hall of Memory on Remembrance Day, 1993.

The outpouring of commemoration included statues, cenotaphs, obelisks, community buildings and more. Major civic memorials like Victoria's massive Shrine of Remembrance, which dominates the southern exit to the city, remain the focus of Anzac Day and Remembrance Day ceremonies. In the embryonic national capital, Canberra, the former journalist Charles Bean, who had laboured tirelessly and bravely as Australia's official war correspondent at Gallipoli and the Western Front, crusaded to commemorate the war dead. He first assembled an enduring paper memorial, writing six volumes of the *Official History of Australia in the War of 1914–18* and editing the remainder. He won national respect as the driving force behind the Australian War Memorial in Canberra, which opened on Remembrance Day 1941 as Australians were again embroiled in war. Commemorating 102,000 Australian war dead, it combines a shrine, a world-class museum, and an extensive archive. 'Here is their spirit, in the heart of the land they loved; and here we guard the record which they themselves made', Bean wrote of the domed building on the central axis of Canberra's formal geometry. It is Australia's most visited museum or gallery, drawing more than 800,000 people annually.

Hundreds of communities complemented their stone memorials with living memorials, avenues of trees planted along major roads leading into the town. While many were created mid-WWI to encourage enlistment and honour volunteers, they inevitably became linear memorials, some with trees bearing individual soldiers' plaques. About three-quarters of these Avenues of Honour are in Victoria. The greatest of around 200 Victorian Avenues of Honour is at Ballarat, where 3,771 trees line 22km of the Western Highway. Jean McAuslan of Victoria's Shrine of Remembrance calls these avenues 'icons of our cultural landscape … rank is typically disregarded and the plaques usually bear only name and initials. The trees came to symbolise community, lives lost, honour, the future denied the dead, and those who grieved their loss.' Perhaps one in four Victorian avenues have faded into the landscape.

Many of those who returned were scarred in mind or body. Children might grow to maturity before appreciating that a father's alcoholism, outbursts of anger or remoteness were linked to the lingering mental or physical costs of war service. In that stoic era, it was unmanly to show weakness; 'shell shock' was a vague description for what would later be diagnosed and described in different terms, including post traumatic stress.

Communities had to adjust to seeing mutilated men, living memorials to war, some reduced to begging. Billboards on public transport reminded people to give a seat to anybody wearing a prominent AIF (later TPI) badge denoting someone Totally and Permanently Incapacitated from war service. The seriously impaired often found their final retreat in one of the Repat (Repatriation) Hospitals or former mansions requisitioned for thousands shattered in mind or body.

Many impacts were unseen. Scotch College historian Dr Jim Mitchell wrote in *The Deepening Roar*: 'More difficult to talk about was the fact that those who came back had killed (or tried to) ... from the 1920s to 1985 the school was dominated by men who while they had not made the supreme sacrifice, had made that other sacrifice: a deliberate decision to break the Sixth Commandment. The effect on these men must have shaped their lives—and shaped the school.'

The College was to retain its martial spirit. Cadets soldier on at Scotch College, one of 223 Australian schools (and community-based bodies) to support almost 15,000 cadets in 2009, compared with a peak of 42,000 in 1966 during the Cold War period. The cadet band is resplendent in kilts.

Faced with a family and community that could not comprehend their war experiences, many returned soldiers found some solace and understanding with former comrades in ex servicemen's clubs (now The Returned and Services League, RSL).

Australia's 1,300 RSL clubs with their 190,000 members continue a nightly tradition, once called, in military parlance, the 'Six o'clock stand-to'. Activity halts for a brief silence, perhaps with lights dimmed. Members may recite lines from Laurence Binyon's 1914 poem *For The Fallen*, familiar from Remembrance ceremonies:

> They shall grow not old, as we that are left grow old:
> Age shall not weary them, nor the years condemn.
> At the going down of the sun and in the morning,
> We will remember them.

They conclude 'Lest We Forget'.

***

Such was the collective response to national loss.

So how did the highly-decorated Alec Little, our most successful fighter pilot, become an unknown warrior to ordinary Australians?

Vera had made the pilgrimage to his grave in France. She later sailed to Australia, by way of Canada, where she had a reunion with his former Squadron Leader, Raymond Collishaw, later to rise to high rank in Canada's air force.

Little did, in fact, receive significant formal recognition. The Australian War Memorial, for instance, displayed relics donated by his descendants in 1978 near mementos of the best known of all fighter pilots, the Red Baron—Manfred von Richthofen. The Museum recently created a permanent exhibition *Over The Front: The Great War in the air*. Looming over Anzac Hall are Allied aircraft (SE5a fighter, Airco DH9 bomber, Avro 504K trainer) and two German fighters brought to Australia in 1919, an Albatros D.Va. and a Pfalz D.XII. One exhibition case displays Little's medals, his temporary wooden grave cross brought to Australia by Vera, a portrait and a few paragraphs on his achievements. A spectacular 12-minute film projected on a curved screen 21 metres by three metres moves from documentary footage to scenes of a squadron of replica SE5s, then into dramatic computer-generated images of combat created by noted director Peter Jackson.

But you will look in vain for R. A. Little on the Roll of Honour which surrounds the Memorial's Commemorative Courtyard. Here are inscribed in bronze the names of virtually every Australian who has died in war in an Australian force since 1885 — more than 102,000 people. Red poppies became a symbol of remembrance after the Great War; on this chilling sweep of marble and bronze, paper poppies, like so many blood spatters, mark visitors' memorialisation of individuals.

Little is, however, on the Commemorative Roll listing Australians who died while members of Allied forces, the merchant navy, philanthropic organisations, as war correspondents, artists and photographers, and certain munition and other workers .

Canberra has other memorials to Little. At the Australian Defence Force Academy, which also holds documents donated by Little's descendants, one of the accommodation blocks is named for him. You will need a map to find it; the large Little building sign has gone missing (2008), although a brass plaque at its entrance still outlines his exploits.

Canberra's planners favoured themed street names. At Scullin, for instance, you navigate curved streets named for noted pilots. There is a splendid irony that in the search for Little, one approach takes you along the sweeping Kingsford Smith Drive (named after Australia's most famous pilot), along Ulm St (Charles Ulm, best known as Kingsford Smith's co-pilot on his trailblazing Pacific flight) and Hinkler St (Bert Hinkler, another aviation pioneer remembered for the 1928 first solo flight to Australia from Britain). You eventually come on neighbouring dead-end streets named for Little and his fellow Ace and friend Major Roderick Dallas.

Late one sunny Spring afternoon, with blossom bright around the 12 homes in Little Place, I found five people at home. None had heard of the deeds of Robert Alexander Little.

Victoria commemorated its Great War dead with the massive granite Shrine of Remembrance, a dominant landmark. Notwithstanding some bitter debates over its very creation (might not a hospital, for example, be more useful?) and its design competition, Sir John

Monash, the Returned Servicemen s League and others eventually succeeded in having it built. Some 300,000 people went to its dedication on Remembrance Day 1934, and it has since been the heart of commemorations on Anzac Day and Remembrance Day.

At a time when very few Victorians could afford a pilgrimage to Europe to seek relatives in the hundreds of Commonwealth War Graves cemeteries springing up across France, Belgium and beyond, it served as a local focus of loss. Its architects included elements from the Parthenon, and a pyramidal roof inspired by the Mausoleum at Halicarnassus in Turkey, one of the seven ancient Wonders of the World.

To many Victorians, the Dawn Service at the Shrine on Anzac Day is a near-religious experience, retaining its impact even as the generations pass.

A small instance of its emotional intensity: as a young reporter covering the Dawn Service in the early 1960s, I saw in the near-darkness a small group of men younger than the WWII veterans. Korea, I asked? Can I have your names? Six Christian names were offered, and written down. Sorry, I said, it's a bit dark, I can see only four of you. The others are still there, was the laconic response.

The names of the Little brothers are in the Shrine's books of remembrance for 89,000 Victorians who served in the Great War. Alec Little is in the Sundry book for those who served in Allied forces.

***

At Point Cook, where Alec had applied unsuccessfully to join Australia's first military pilots, the Australian Flying Corps Memorial of 1938 is inclusive. Honouring Australian aviators who died in the Great War, it includes those who joined British services.

At Scotch College, loyalty to Britain had remained fierce. An example was the first Private W. L. Colclough Prize awarded for a song by a Scotch student. The winning song, by I. R. Maxwell, proved very successful, a school history noted.

To the tune *Men of Harlech*, young Maxwell's *Australian Battle Song* included the lines

> See the banners streaming;
> See the bright steel gleaming;
> Rouse ye all at England's call,
> Blood your trust redeeming.
> Where the battle parts asunder,
> Tread the yielding foeman under,
> Hurl this shout beyond the thunder—
> Death or Victory!
> ... Names of those who died for Britain
> Honoured evermore!

Those who died for Britain would be honoured at Scotch, where the war had taken a monstrous toll. Post-war, as the school expanded on its new 50-acre hillside site at Hawthorn, the names of 204 old boys who did not return would be placed at the front of the Memorial Hall.

Its fundraisers spoke of 'Our Valhalla', Norse mythology's great hall of heroes killed in battle. There is a different mythology in the blaze of heraldry in its six stained glass windows above the names of the Great War dead, a dramatic expression of the religious and patriotic commemoration of the era. At left, St Andrew, Patron Saint of Scotland—the only figure not in medieval armour—and St Martin, whose feast day is 11 November (Remembrance Day). Centre, below the Rising Sun emblem of the AIF, is King Arthur (whose existence is a long running historical debate) and Sir Galahad, renowned for gallantry as one of the legendary Knights of the Round Table.

At right, St Michael, the militant archangel, and St George, patron saint of England, familiar as the dragon slayer.

The History of Scotch College 1851–1921 claimed Little 'had gained much promotion, and refused more, as he could not face the job of sending others up to do the fighting. Though little more than a boy, Flight-Commander R. A.Little's fame was blazoned in the sky. A better fighter never lived.' The legend was forming.

He flew with the school colours behind his plane, the story went. But while Little, air fighter par excellence, would be mentioned in school histories, a former Scotch College dux would emerge from the disastrous war as the college's best-known graduate. General Sir John Monash, civil engineer and peacetime soldier, rose to command the Australian Corps in France during some of the climactic battles of the war.

Monash applied his civil engineer's skills to the military arts, focussed on using technology to save the lives of his men. With meticulous planning, especially collaboration across the services, he became one of the Allies' most respected generals.

As post-war head of Victoria's State Electricity Commission, he used liberated German brown coal technology to open the immense reserves of Victoria's Latrobe Valley for generation of cheap electricity. Who could guess that brown coal would eventually be reviled as a major source of the carbon dioxide linked to climate change, key to another form of global war?

His name was given to Victoria's second university, an outer Melbourne council, a freeway and more than 30 other streets, a large public hospital and much more. His fame endures; he is on Australia's $100 banknote.

By comparison, Little's fame was fleeting.

Barely a month after the killing had stopped, Victoria's Solicitor General (and Scotch College Old Boy), The Honourable Arthur Robinson, orated in full patriotic flight at the college speech night at Melbourne Town Hall. He borrowed some newspaper phrases.

Excerpts: 'The total record of the College in man power and brain power is, I believe, unapproached by that of any school in the Dominions ... the Commander in Chief of the AIF is a former Dux of the college ... the Australian forces in England trained under another Dux, Sir J. W. McKay ...

'Of others of whom we can hardly think without risk of break-down, who 'poured out the red sweet wine of youth' in the nation's cause', he cited two. The school vice-captain in 1914, and former editor of the school paper, James Burns, had written the widely-recognised clarion-call poem *(The bugles of England were blowing o'er the sea)* which had inspired many a young Australian beyond the walls of the college. His life at the college was manly and clean, his conscience clear and his courage high, the Solicitor General intoned. Corporal Burns had died on Gallipoli in 1915.

'Then came Bob Little ... the deeds of no airman in the whole war exceed this Scotch College boy's for valour, for coolness, for daring. In his short life honours were heaped upon him as some small tokens of his country's and its Allies' admiration ...

'But the distinction dearest to us is that he insisted on his favourite airplane being painted in Scotch College colours. And further, and still more touching, which stirs the deepest feelings and must move the more unemotional, are the instructions he left that, if death did befall him, his infant son in due course should become a Scotch Collegian. Bob Little wrote his name in letters of glory in the heavens, and died on the wings of fame.'

Thus are legends born and sustained. While there are no records of Little having painted his plane in school colours (the RNAS stuck to dark brown), his widow Vera noted decades later that he had, once only, flown streamers in school colours from his wingtips while a Flight Sub Lieutenant.

The hero's son, whose nickname BLYMP was painted large on the fuselage of his father's Sopwith Triplane, was never to go to Scotch College. After moving to Melbourne, mother and son initially lived on St Kilda Road, main southern exit from the city, opposite Wesley College. Young Alec attended Wesley.

***

Alec Little is remembered on British memorials. In London, he is on the rolls of honour at St Clement Danes in the Strand, the central church of the Royal Air Force. It was restored after being burned out in the 1940 Blitz by a more potent generation of German bombers.

At the Royal Air Force Museum at Hendon, you can see Little's restored Sopwith Pup N8152, the former *Lady Maud*. The accompanying display board, *Aussie Pups*, notes that formidable air fighters such as Captain R. A. Little ... flew the type' but does not identify this as Little's actual aircraft.

Post-war, the remains of the Pup were stored for decades in a former French airship hangar as part of the Musée de l'Air reserve collection. The late Lt Cdr K. C. D. (Desmond) St Cyrien MBE, a former Royal Navy pilot, somehow obtained the relics—a heap of parts with its 80hp Le Rhone engine, and the wings and fuselage, with the remains of fabric. It lacked machinegun, instruments and undercarriage. St Cyrien launched a 13-year restoration, acquiring some instruments and parts from the original Pup prototype, the carburettor from Brussels Museum, the BTH Magneto from Finland and pair of Pup wheels from a handcart in Lincoln. The Vickers Museum at Weybridge provided a machinegun, the Birmingham Science Museum a Lang propeller. Much of the original ash in the longerons and wing spars was replaced and the engine was rebuilt by the Royal Aircraft Establishment. The RAF Museum notes say the Pup is supposedly 60–70 per cent original, or at least has contemporary components. Britain's Civil Aviation Authority accepted it as genuine only after they received a letter to that effect from the legendary aircraft designer Sir Thomas Sopwith, born 1888, whose company built the Pup at Kingston upon Thames in 1916. Sir Thomas lived to 101.

A veteran pilot, Neil Williams, made flight tests, including a forced landing during the delivery flight. Little would have laughed.

The Pup was flown at air shows at Biggin Hill and Old Warden before Williams flew it for 25 minutes at Honington on 25 October 1976 for the Diamond Jubilee of 8 Squadron RNAS, now 208 Squadron RAF. With some 10 hours flying time after its resurrection, it was eventually acquired by the Museum in 1982 for immediate display in its WWI collection.

***

Walmer, Kent, late November 2009: Commander John May, a Royal Navy veteran, often walks his dog past the RNAS memorial on this former farmland which served as Walmer Aerodrome in 1917–1918. As vice-chairman of the local Royal British Legion (ex-service association, equivalent to the Australian RSL) he is quietly pleased to see that Remembrance Day commemorations have extended even to this remote memorial. It bears a wreath from the Rotary Club of Deal, and four unnamed small wooden crosses.

The lives of two Australians proud of their Scots ancestry, both eminent in their own spheres, intersected at Walmer.

Alec (sometimes called Bob) Little earned a chestful of military decorations. His name is on the memorial to the 15 Great War RNAS and RAF pilots who had served at Walmer, and died on active service.

Bob Menzies, as Australians commonly called him, had a wealth of civilian honours: Sir Robert Gordon Menzies, KT, AK, CH, FRS, QC was Australia's longest-serving Prime Minister and a staunch supporter of Australia's ties to Britain. In 1965 he succeeded Sir Winston Churchill as Lord Warden of the Cinque Ports, the first time in 900 years that this post had been given to someone from overseas. The Lord Warden's official residence is at Walmer Castle, just below the site of the former airfield—and one of Sir Robert's predecessors here erected the memorial to the RNAS pilots in 1920.

The Kent coast has been an actual and potential invasion route for 2000 years. Tourists and military archaeologists alike marvel at the overlay of structures reflecting man's propensity to violence, often at the same strategic river crossings or coastal high points. Roman forts; the castles with which William the Conquerer's descendants consolidated their successful invasion of 1066; the unusual artillery forts—with a ground plan rather like a four-leaf clover—which Henry VIII built to keep the Spaniards at bay following the Armada of 1588; the scores of small circular Martello Towers built to repel a Napoleonic beach assault; the more low-profile fortifications built to resist breech-loading guns in the 19th and 20th centuries, and myriad pillboxes from 1939–40.

One of the romantic tales of English military history is that of the Cinque Ports, Norman French for five ports. Hastings, New Romney, Hythe, Dover, and Sandwich, coastal towns in Kent and Sussex at the narrowest part of the English Channel, formed a military and trade alliance dating from the 12th Century. The position of Lord Warden of the Cinque Ports, long a ceremonial office, is one of the higher honours that a British sovereign can bestow. While Sir Robert's elaborate and archaic uniform was a Gilbert & Sullivan cartoonist's delight, Australians were generally appreciative of the honour, and Sir Robert certainly performed his ceremonial tasks with enthusiasm during annual summer visits.

Alec Little's interment in France, behind a Casualty Clearing Station, was necessarily basic. With padres often attached to such grim places, there may have been some brief words before his body was committed to what the English poet Rupert Brooke called in 1914 '… some corner of a foreign field / That is forever England.'

The dedication of the memorial to Little and his RNAS and RAF comrades on 7 August 1920 was rather more splendid, performed with the pomp and ceremony at which the English excel.

'It was a beautiful August evening, the rays of the setting sun casting their glow on the wooded grounds of Walmer Castle, and on the ripe grain of the cornfields in Walmer's charming Glen, as a representative company assembled,' enthused the journalist from the *East Kent Mercury*.

The memorial by the edge of the former airfield was erected by the Countess Beauchamp, wife of Earl Beauchamp, Lord Warden of the Cinque Ports. 'It was in a railed enclosure facing the Downs, over which roadstead the gallant airmen so often flew in the course of their duty to protect this vitally important examination anchorage from air attacks,' the report noted.

From the castle grounds a procession made its way across Hawks' Hill to the site of the memorial. A cross-bearer walked first, followed by two robed clergy, the Chaplain-in-Chief, Royal Air Force, and the Vicar of Walmer, Rev. N. C. W. Radcliffe. Earl Beauchamp, in the uniform of the Lord Warden of the Cinque Ports, was with Air-Commodore C. L. Lambe, CMG, DSO, who unveiled the memorial.

The guard of honour was called to attention as Air Commodore Lambe removed the Union Jack covering the memorial, with the words: 'In the faith of Jesus Christ I unveil this memorial, to the greater glory of God and in memory of those officers of the Royal Naval Air Service and the Royal Air Force who served at Walmer aerodrome, and who gave their lives for their King and Country in the Great War.'

Air Commodore Lambe outlined the history of the aerodrome. Hymns were sung, prayers read. 'Four buglers of the Queen's Cadets marched to the front of the guard-of-honour, who came to the Slope Arms position, and the sounding of the "Last Post", followed by the singing of "God Save The King". Wreaths were deposited on the memorial steps by Lady Beauchamp and by Mrs Little, accompanied by her boy.'

Flight magazine of August 12, 1920 also noted the presence of 'Lord and Lady George Hamilton, Lady Helen Grosvenor, Lord Elmley, the Ladies Lettice, Sibell, Mary, and Dorothy Lygon, daughters of Lord Beauchamp, Lady Sargent, and Sir William Pearce MP and Lady Pearce.'

Altogether an impressive and touching service, the *East Kent Mercury* added.

The memorial with the names of the pilots, and patriotic and religious verses, has largely survived the ravages of time. Much of the aerodrome site is now Hawkshill Freedown, a 13.7-acre public open space designated a *Site of Nature Conservation Interest* reflecting its national importance for wildlife, particularly wildflowers and butterflies.

It provides superb views across open farmland to shipping in the English Channel, the Goodwin Sands and, on a clear day, the French coast 21 miles distant which was the last landfall of so many young pilots. While the original thatched roof of the memorial has long been replaced, volunteers (most recently members of the

South Foreland Rotary Club in 2005) have helped Walmer Parish Council to clean up, replant and repaint the memorial, and keep vegetation at bay.

When the wind blows across the Downs, it is not difficult to imagine the buzz of engines here, and the years when there were biplane hawks above Hawks' Hill Farm.

Sir Robert Menzies, often seen as the last bold figure of Anglo Australia, once described himself as 'British to the Bootstraps'. The devoted Royalist must have known of the pilots' memorial; whether he made it up the hill, and was aware that Little was Australian, is unknown.

Sir Robert was at Melbourne University doing Law (and in the Melbourne University Rifles) when Little was at war, but did not volunteer. With his two elder brothers already serving, a family conference decided that he should stay. Later bitter political taunts of shirker seem less than fair play.

With his Scots heritage in evidence to the last, the gruff political warrior received a State Funeral at Scots Church in Melbourne in 1978, 60 years to the month after Little's death. At Springvale crematorium his funeral cortege was met by a lone piper who led the coffin into the chapel, playing the traditional Scottish lament 'The Flowers of the Forest'.

***

Notwithstanding the various official commemorations, and rare newspaper features, Little has vanished from the appreciation of almost all Australians, excepting military historians and aviation enthusiasts. His death on that May night in 1918 ended any chance of post-war fame, such as that hard won by aviation trailblazers like Western Front survivors Kingsford Smith or Hinkler, or as a possible career officer in the RAAF, like the Australian Flying Corps highest-scoring pilot, Harry Cobby, who rose to Air Commodore in WWII. There would be no memoirs like Cobby's *High Adventure*. Nor would he have the chance, decades on, to revisit the Western

Front airfields reverted to farmland as Sir Gordon Taylor did half a century later in preparation for his memoir *Sopwith Scout 7309*, which memorably captures the precarious life of the fighter pilot.

In an omission sometimes criticised, the hundreds of Australians who joined foreign services (usually because they could not get into Australia's embryonic air force early in the war) missed out in the first editions of Frederick Morley Cutlack's Volume VIII of the official history, *Australian Flying Corps*. Its introduction stated 'The fortunes of the Australian airmen who served [in foreign forces] cannot be followed in a history of the purely Australian Flying Corps.' (The history found space for a two-page appendix on the ethics and efficiency of various incendiary and explosive bullets.)

The third edition relaxed this policy and incorporated a modest footnote with some names of those who had served outside Australian squadrons; the list was expanded for the fourth edition of 1935, where the greatest of all Australian fighting pilots appears as footnote 40 on page xxvi:

> Capt. R. A. Little. D.S.O., D.S.C. No. 203 Sqn. R.A.F.
> (Previously No. 3, R.N.A.S.) Of Melbourne; b. 19 July,
> 1895. Killed in action, 27 May, 1918.

Many people thought the non-AFC airmen deserved better. As recently as 2002, an article on Little in the Victorian RSL Magazine, *Mufti*, concluded 'thanks to the official Australian historians, he took his fame to the grave with him.'

***

The tower of the imposing Australian National War Memorial rises from the fields outside Villers–Bretonneux where the Diggers helped stem the last major German offensive of the war. It is far removed in scale and memorial architecture from the modest Wavans War Cemetery.

The Memorial was dedicated on 22 July 1938 by King George VI of Britain in the presence of Albert Lebrun, President of France, Earl Page, Deputy Prime Minister of Australia, and a large crowd. It has long been a setting for formal Anzac Day commemoration by a relative handful of diplomatic, political and military dignitaries and visitors gathered before walls incised with the names of 11,000 Australian soldiers with no known grave.

Only recently, with Australians moving beyond the preoccupation with Gallipoli to recognise the far greater toll of Australia's three years on the Western Front, has the memorial attracted significant Anzac Day crowds. The Dawn Service was first televised live to Australia in 2008 and the service currently attracts around 4,000 people.

One of the headstones you see on the approach to the Memorial honours a Western Australian farmer, Sgt Phillip James Ball, winner of a Military Medal while serving with the 44th Battalion. He died aged 23 on 28 March 1918.

His next of kin crafted an inscription far from the typical family, religious or patriotic themes:

> I FOUGHT AND DIED
> IN THE GREAT WAR
> TO END ALL WARS.
> HAVE I DIED IN VAIN?

Fair question. Less than two years after its dedication, the Memorial was scarred by bullets from the German blitzkrieg of 1940. The Great War which had consumed so many was soon to be retitled World War 1 in the catalogue of 20th century conflict.

Epilogue

A land fit for heroes?

The Great War convulsed nations, sundered Empires, and affected the lives of generations of survivors and their families.

Some people suspected very early that the Armistice represented unfinished business. On 13 May 1919 the *Daily Herald* of London ran a famously prescient political cartoon by Will Dyson, who had been an Australian official war artist. '*Peace and future cannon fodder*' showed the French Prime Minister, Georges Clemenceau, (nicknamed 'The Tiger') and the three other peacemakers leaving after crafting the Treaty of Versailles. Unseen behind a pillar is the crying figure of a child tagged '1940 class'—the crop of young men who would come into military maturity for the mass armies of Europe in that year. The caption: *The Tiger: 'Curious! I seem to hear a child weeping'.*

During the 1918 UK election campaign, Prime Minister David Lloyd George memorably declared that the postwar world 'must be a land fit for heroes to live in'. But hard economic times, culminating in the Depression, ensured the phrase soon rang hollow. Today we still use it to mock grandiose promises unlikely to be honoured. Many Australians might apply it, for instance, to the well-meaning but poorly-thought-through post-war Soldier Settlement schemes, where too many former city dwellers came to grief trying to survive on rural blocks too small for efficient farming.

The Little family, like so many worldwide, also fell on hard times.

James Little had suffered the death of his wife Susy in late 1915, and apprehension for both sons at war. While the return of his younger son eased one worry, the father's fears for his pilot son continued through 1916, 1917 and 1918. He admired Alec's bravery and growing toll of enemy aircraft, publicly recognised by a swag of medals; he passed at least one of Alec's letters from the front to Scotch College for publication in the school magazine. Alec's marriage, and the arrival of his grandson Alec, would have been another distraction from the mounting casualty lists.

He provided background for news stories on his multiple medal awards ... and eventually for his obituaries.

The family's ill fortune continued post-war. James the Gallipoli veteran resumed life as a salesman, married twice, but had no children. He died of heart disease, age 40, at Balmoral Beach in Sydney on 8 January 1938. Information for his death certificate came from his widow, then living in New Zealand.

The oldest of the four siblings, Sylvia Clow Little, was 22 when she married Dr James Webb, 20 years her senior, in March 1916. She seems something of a free spirit—or an inheritor of the wanderlust gene that had taken the Little bloodline from Scotland to Canada and to Australia.

In 1923 *The Argus* reported that Dr Webb had successfully petitioned for divorce on the ground of desertion. Webb told the Divorce Court that before they were married, Sylvia told him of an inclination to go on the stage; when he suggested there would be little point marrying, she abandoned the idea. Soon after the marriage, while he was away on professional business, he learned she had joined the John O'Hara Lightnin' Company. He later saw his wife in Sydney, where she was then playing, but could not persuade her to quit the stage. He told the court she was living in Capital Avenue, New York, and had gone through a form of marriage.

The patriarch James Little died at 71 of kidney disease on 6 December 1933. He was spared another war death, that of his grandson Robert Alexander (Alick) Shmith, only child of the first marriage of Dorothy, youngest of the four Little children.

Dorothy had given her firstborn the Christian names of her late pilot brother. Alick, an Acting Bombardier with the Royal Australian

Artillery, was 21 when was killed in action at Tobruk in North Africa on 15 June 1941. During the siege, German propaganda derided the defenders as rats in a hole, perhaps not appreciating Australians' enthusiasm for bestowing offensive nicknames. The Australians thereafter called themselves 'The Rats of Tobruk', turning an insult into a badge of honour.

Dorothy told John Bruce Bingeman, her only child by her second marriage, that Alick was a conscientious objector serving as a stretcher bearer. He was Mentioned in Dispatches.

John Bingeman has childhood memories of Dorothy speaking fondly of Alec Little as a great hero. 'He certainly seems a little undersung' is his wry comment on Little's lack of recognition.

***

And what of the widow Vera and her son Alec?

Post-war, the Scotch College magazine said Alec and Vera had a pact that if he died, she and their child would join his family in Melbourne. They stayed briefly in Melbourne, at James Little's home in Punt Rd, Windsor, returning to London on the *City of Karachi* on 30 January 1919.

In May 1920, while living at Dover, Vera received a letter from Friedrich Neumuller, the German airman forced down by Alec on 24 April 1917 and subsequently entertained by the squadron.

Neumuller made his condolences and praised his captor as

> a clever and brave pilot and not only during that combat, but also, when I was his prisoner, an adversary, very honourable and noble.
>
> That my last air battle will ever leave in my memory a profound admiration for him. I had hoped that he was, perhaps, still alive, but I got the information that he was killed in action in the field.
>
> Because—as the victorious enemy—he was so amiable to me on the darkest day of my soldierly life, I will never forget

him. We both did not hate us fighting each other, but we
both did only our duty, he for his King and Country, and I
for my Kaiser and Fatherland.
I should be very obliged to you when you will kindly send me
a picture of your late husband, in ever respecting memory of
my knightly adversary in the air.

An English newspaper reprinted the letter, a reminder of the
chivalry sometimes associated with the first fighter pilots. Vera sent
a photograph of Little to Neumuller, who became a pastor after the
war. He sent Vera and Alec a Christmas card each year, and their
regular correspondence, interrupted only by WWII, continued
until his death a few years after the war.

Vera and Alec laid a wreath at the dedication of the RNAS
Memorial at Walmer in August 1920. They returned to Melbourne
on the *Mooltan* from Marseilles on 23 January 1924. Among
Vera's belongings was a hexagonal jewel case made by squadron
mechanics from timber from Alec's wrecked aircraft, with a tunic
button inset, and the inscription *Izel Le Hameau, 1918*.

In July 1925, Vera married a British ex-serviceman. Her
descendants recall that the living room wall over the piano in her
home at Elwood in Melbourne was long dominated by the wooden
propeller given to Vera by her husband's squadron mates after
Alec's death. The propeller, which the family believe is from his
Triplane, is now stored at the Australian War Memorial, a clock
inset in its hub with its hours marked by cartridges.

In 1927 Vera paid the Imperial War Graves Commission to ship
Alec's temporary wooden grave cross to her.

The pilot was always 'the ghost in the house', one descendant
recalls. Vera was known to say 'Alec should have won the VC.' In
March 1937, writing to the WWI historian Charles Bean with an
outline of Alec Little's career, Vera had concluded: 'We hear so
much of all these German and French Aces, yet he was truly an
Australian Ace, never heard of.'

Vera retained an English reserve, and an English accent. Finances were often tight.

Young Alec became a respected technician, heading the electronics workshop at the School of Physics at Melbourne University, moving beyond the vacuum tube era into early experiments with computers. His former boss, Professor David Caro, admired Alec's dedication, notably with 'a long bank of electronics which functioned in a way similar to a modern computer…it rarely operated for long before a part failed.' Other former colleagues recalled him as a gentle, reclusive and shy man who lived at home with his mother. Alec once visited the UK to help settle his grandmother's estate. He never married, and lived with his mother.

He left work one day in 1976 after hearing that his mother was sick. An angina sufferer for years, he died of a heart attack that day at the foot of her bed on 25 August, aged 59.

A year and a day later, on 26 August 1977, Vera died at 83 of bronchopneumonia. She had had a stroke two months before.

In 1978 Vera's descendants donated the family's relics and documents of Robert Alexander Little to the Australian War Memorial and the Australian Defence Force Academy. On the rear of the shield-shaped presentation case displaying his medals is scratched '*Given to my Blymp from Mumsie, 1918*' and '*Blymp Little, 1918*'.

One descendant has a gift from a friend on her TV—a small teddy bear wearing old-fashioned pilot's helmet and goggles, sheepskin jacket and white scarf. 'Biggles', she jokes.

Her final judgment on Alec? 'Brave but reckless.' Who would disagree?

Acknowledgments

In search of a hero

Alec Little spent his early years in the Melbourne suburb of Hawthorn, as did my father.

The search for Alec was indirectly triggered by my father's command of 14 Platoon, 2/24th Battalion, in Posts S10, S11 and S11a in the 'Rats of Tobruk' perimeter defences of this strategic port in Mussolini's former North African empire in May 1941.

As part of the seesaw battles along the Mediterranean coast, with control of the Suez Canal the prize, General Erwin Rommel's Afrika Korps had pursued retreating Australian and British troops to Tobruk.

At the far end of his supply line, Rommel made a bold last raid with a handful of panzers to attempt to seize what was optimistically called Fortress Tobruk. But this 'Easter Battle' was hardly the blitzkrieg that had won all in Poland and France.

The German and Italian tanks which penetrated the defences soon lost momentum against British 25-pounder field guns. When the Afrika Korps retreated, relieving troops worried about the fate of the Australian forward units on the edge of the assault found that Lt John Rosel and his men had managed to defend their posts. The former Hawthorn bank clerk won a Military Cross. The citation spoke in part of 'calm and outstanding leadership… his platoon fought off repeated attacks…continued to hold posts against repeated attacks'.

And that was all his six children would ever know of what men did to other men in those violent hours in their desert weapon pits. Even in the most intimate chats, he always gently deflected questions about combat. His children were to find it was a near-universal response by returned soldiers.

As youngsters, we went to a few Battalion picnics, where inarticulate strangers would pat us on the head and say nice things about my father. But I cannot remember him going to Anzac Day marches, or (a non-drinker) to a RSL club.

Seeking enlightenment, I started to read on military matters, by way of Stephen Crane, *All Quiet on the Western Front*, Shakespeare, Russell Braddon, the war poets, *The Naked and The Dead*, Chester Wilmot, and much more ... even *Winged Victory*, a brilliant, bleak semi-autobiographical novel of Great War air combat by a Camel pilot, Victor Yeates. It was a serious corrective to the ripping-yarn *Biggles* books for young people by another Great War pilot, Capt W. E. Johns.

With family forbearance, I walked battlefields from Quebec to Gettysburg, from Fort Douamont at Verdun to more recent killing fields in Vietnam, from Hadrian's Wall to Australia's civil insurrection at the gold rush Eureka Stockade in Victoria, from Villers-Bretonneux to Mouquet Farm, from France's only concentration camp (Natzweiler-Struthof) to the Army base at Puckapunyal in central Victoria, where my father's generation had trained, and where his sons in school cadets handled identical weapons.

Gallipoli proved a numbing two days. The Dawn Service, with a moon low over the Aegean from whence the young men had come to the wrong beach on 25 April 1915, was anguish across the pilgrim generations. Later, at Lone Pine, young people chided by some for their generation's clamorous contributions to commemorative services, were struck silent as they emerged from the building housing the books of remembrance. A common scrawl there was 'those poor bastards'.

***

A quick visit to the RAF Museum at Hendon in May 2008, with the assistance of education officer Vernon Creek, took a surprising turn when he pointed out a beautifully-restored Sopwith Pup of 1916.

A display panel *('Aussie' Pups)* mentioned some 'formidable fighter pilots who had flown the type, including Captain R. A. Little (47 claims).' Not being a Great War aviation expert, the name did not ring a bell to me.

Vernon dug out the museum's background notes on the small aircraft—and it proved to be Little's first fighter! Back in Australia, it became obvious that while Little was well-documented by the military and aviation historians, scores of questions among friends and acquaintances suggested he was unknown to the ordinary Australian. Hence the search for a hero.

At Scotch College, history teacher and military historian Dr Mark Johnston gave me basic references and introduced me to College archivist Dr Jim Mitchell and colleague Paul Mishura, who guided me through school records and Edwardian-era copies of *The Scotch Collegian*. Mark also headed off text errors.

The Australian War Memorial and the Australian Defence Force Academy were generous in making available Little material, and offering follow-up advice. Particular thanks to Nick Fletcher, Craig Tibbetts and Kerrie Leech at the AWM, and Wilgha Edwards at the ADFA Library. Professor Melanie Nolan, Director, National Centre for Biography, Australian National University, provided Little background. At the Fleet Air Arm museum at Nowra, New South Wales, curator Ailsa Chittick provided valuable information and a Little photograph never previously published.

On a 2009 visit to London, I was guided through the National Archives at Kew by Gerry Toop, saw personal and squadron records, and felt the decades recede as I held some of Little's original combat reports signed just before his death. The UK National Meteorological Library and Archive kindly unearthed weather information for his last flight.

Across the Channel which he had crossed often in those flimsy machines—and thanks to the research and French fluency of an old friend, Barbara Whiteman—I talked to Pierre Geron, the farmer whose land surrounds Wavans war cemetery, and to Daniel Melin, the mayor of the small village of Noeux where Little's last flight ended. Notwithstanding a regional newspaper article on the search, and many word-of-mouth inquiries around the village, the mayor had no luck when asking old-timers if they knew the crash site.

At the Commonwealth War Graves Commission in London, Ranald Leask and colleagues unearthed files from 1918 onwards which outlined how Little came to be buried at Wavans, a tiny element in the vast memorialisation of the dead.

Among many who patiently saved me from a tyro's errors, British aviation historian and author of more than 122 books, Norman Franks, was especially generous, particularly with text permissions from *Cross & Cockade*, thanks also to RAAF Museum Point Cook research curator Monica Walsh, and archivists at Melbourne and suburban libraries.

Descendants of Little, some of whom wish to remain anonymous, recounted family stories of the young man who wanted to fly, and gave insights into the family's postwar fate.

Others who made invaluable contributions included Kim Andrews, friend and genealogist; Tim Graham; the Minifie family; P&O historian Rob Henderson, Sydney; Canberra guide and host Helen Palethorpe; Di Gardiner, Public Records Office, Victoria; Kerri Ward, National Archives of Australia; Commander John May (Walmer), and Paul Taylor, John Tidey, Noel Carrick, Bill Clancy, Jeremy Bourke, Rex Booker, Ian Hicks and Paul Webb. Publisher Nick Walker and team teased everything together.

A final irony and comment on the futility of war: At Hawthorn, where the stories of Little and my father intersect briefly, a 77mm German trophy field gun from the Great War pointed for half a century at an Australian office of the Commonwealth War Graves Commission, a few yards away at the other end of the bridge from Richmond.

Mike Rosel
Armadale, Victoria
2012

Little's 47 claims [courtesy Norman Franks]

				PUP		
1916						
1	23 Nov	C-type two seater	N5182	1m NE La Bassee	Destroyed (in flames)
2	4 Dec	Halb. DII	N5182	NE Bapaume	Out of control
3	20 Dec	C-type two seater	N5182	Fontaine	Out of control
1917						
4	7 Jan	Alb. DII	N5182	Grevillers	Out of control
				TRIPLANE		
5	7 April	Alb.DIII	N5469	SE Lens	Destroyed
6	9 April	Halb.DII	N5469	Noyelles/Lens	Out of control
7	21 April	Alb. DIII	N5469	NE Oppy	Destroyed
8*	24 April	Aviatik two seater	N5469	Auchel	Captured
9	28 April	C-type two seater	N5493	Oppy	Destroyed
10*	29 April	Alb.DIII	N5493	Douai	Destroyed
11	30 April	Alb. DIII	N5493	E Arras	Out of control
12	30 April	Alb.DIII	N5493	E Arras	Out of control
13	2 May	Alb. DIII	N5493	Vitry	Out of control
14	9 May	LVG two seater	N5493	SE Lens	Out of control
15	9 May	Alb. DIII	N5493	SE Lens	Out of control
16	10 May	Alb.DIII	N5493	Lens	Out of control
17	18 May	DFW two seater	N5493	NE Lens	Destroyed
18	18 May	Alb. DIII	N5493	NE Lens	Destroyed
19*	23 May	Alb.DIII	N5493	W Douai	Out of control
20	25 May	Alb. DIII	N5493	Quiery la Motte	Out of control
21*	16 June	C-type two seater	N5493	Wingles	Destroyed
22	21 June	Alb.DV	N5493	E Henin-Lietard	Destroyed
23	26 June	C-type two seater	N5493	1m E Acheville	Destroyed (in flames)
24*	29 June	Alb.DV	N5493	E Lens	Out of control
25	3 July	Alb.DV	N5493	Lens	Out of control
26	3 July	Alb.DV	N5493	Lens-La Bassee	Out of control
27	6 July	C-type two seater	N5493	N Izel	Destroyed
28	10 July	Alb.DV	N5493	Fampoux	Out of control
				CAMEL		
29	12 July	Alb.DV	N6378	Vitry-Drocourt-Queant	Out of control
30	13 July	C-type two seater	N6378	Lens	Out of control
31	13 July	Alb.DV	N6378	Croiselles	Captured
32	15 July	Alb.DV	N6378	Lens	Out of control

33	16 July	C-type two seater	N6378	Gavrelle	Out of control
34*	20 July	DFW CV	N6378	Lens	Destroyed
35	21 July	Alb.DV	N6378	E. Oppy	Out of control
36	22 July	C-type two seater	N6378	Rouvroy	Out of control
37	22 July	Alb.DV	N6378	Lens	Out of control
38*	27 July	DFW	B3877	Loos	Destroyed

1918

39	1 April	Fokker DrI	B7198	3m E Oppy	Destroyed
40	6 April	DFW CV	B7231	NE Lens	Destroyed (in flames)
41	7 April	Fokker DrI	B7231	1m SE Violanes	Destroyed
42*	9 April	Alb.C	B7231	Givenchy	Destroyed (in flames)
43	11 April	Alb. DV	B7231	Bac St Maur	Destroyed
44	11 April	Alb. DV	B7231	W Bailleul	Out of control
45*	18 May	Pfalz DIII	B7220	Neuf Berquin	Out of control
46	22 May	Alb.C	D3416	Mory–St Leger	Destroyed
47	22 May	DFW. C	D3416	Morchies	Destroyed

* shared

Total: 1 and 1 shared, captured; 17 and 5 shared, destroyed; 21 and 2 shared, out of control : **47**

Medal citations in the London Gazette:

16 February 1917 **Distinguished Service Cross**
Flt. Sub. Lt. Robert Alexander Little, R.N.A.S. For conspicuous bravery in successfully attacking and bringing down hostile machines on several occasions. On 11th November, 1916, he attacked and brought down a hostile machine in flames. On 12th December, 1916, he attacked a German machine at a range of 50 yards; this machine was brought down in a nose dive. On 20th December, 1916, he dived at a hostile machine, and opened fire at 25 yards range; the Observer was seen to fall down inside the machine, which went down in a spinning nose dive. On 1st January, 1917, he attacked an enemy scout, which turned over on its back and came down completely out of control.

22 June 1917 **Bar to Distinguished Service Cross**
Flt. Lieut. Robert Alexander Little, DSC, RNAS. For exceptional daring and skill in air fighting on many occasions, of which the following are examples:-

On 28th April 1917, he destroyed an Aviatik, on the 29th April, he shot down a hostile scout, which crashed. On the 30th April, with three other machines he went up after hostile machines and saw a big fight going on between fighter escorts and hostile aircraft. Flt. Lieut. Little attacked one at fifty yards range, and brought it down out of control. A few minutes later he attacked a red scout with a larger machine than the rest. This machine was handled with great skill, but by clever manoeuvring Flt. Lieut. Little got into a good position and shot it down out of control.

20 July 1917 **Croix de Guerre**
The following decorations have been conferred by the Allied Powers on Officers of the British Naval Forces for distinguished services rendered during the war. Decorations conferred by the President of the French Republic: *Flt. Lieut. Robert A Little, DSC, R.N.A.S.*

11 August 1917 **Companion of the Distinguished Service Order**
Flt. Lieut. Robert Alexander Little, DSC, R.N.A.S. For gallantry in action
and for exceptional skill and daring in aerial combats. Since the 9th
May, 1917, besides having driven off numerous artillery aeroplanes
and damaged six hostile machines, he has destroyed six others. On
the 26th June, 1917, an Aviatik being seen from the aerodrome, he
went up to attack it. He engaged it and fired a burst at close range,
and the enemy machine stalled and went down in flames.

14 September 1917 **Bar to Distinguished Service Order**
Flt. Lieut (Actg. Flt Cdr.) Robert Alexander Little, DSO, DSC, R.N.A.S.
For exceptional gallantry and skill in aerial fighting. On 16th July,
1917, he observed two Aviatiks flying low over the lines. He dived at
the nearest one, firing a long burst at very close range. The enemy
machine dived straight away, and Flt. Lieut. Little followed him
closely down to 500 ft., the enemy machine falling out of control.

On 20th July, 1917, he attacked a D.F.W. after a short fight the
enemy machine dived vertically. The tail plane seemed to crumple
up, and it was completely wrecked.

In 22nd July, 1917, he attacked a D.F.W. aviatik and brought it
down completely out of control.

On 27th July, 1917, in company with another pilot, he attacked
an Aviatik. After each had fired about twenty rounds, the enemy
machine began to spin downwards. Flt. Lieut. Little got close to it,
and observed both the occupants lying back in the cockpits, as if
dead. The machine fell behind the enemy's lines and was wrecked.

Flt. Lieut. Little has shown remarkable courage and boldness in
attacking enemy machines.

11 December, 1917: Flt. Lieut. Little, **Mentioned in Despatches.**

Elegy from a country tip

Alec Little's saga had an astonishing and poignant postscript 93 years after his death on the Western Front.

In southern Queensland—some 1450km north of Little's home town of Melbourne—a Stanthorpe farmer with a collecting bent opened an old Gladstone bag left for potential recycling by the gate of a refuse transfer station near the small town of Texas.

He found mice nesting in an old tweed coat. Discarding the fouled coat, he noted what he thought was an old leather motorcycle helmet and some clothes, before storing the bag in his shed.

Eighteen months later, in July 2013, he remembered the helmet, thinking it might look good on a mannequin's head he had acquired…

At last he explored the bag's contents…an old flying helmet, goggles, clothing, and other relics, many bearing the name 'R.A. Little'.

As he awaited responses to his queries to WWI air combat websites, he discovered something concealed inside the front flap of the helmet. Not wishing to damage the leather, he had his local vet take an x-ray. The vet confirmed a strange object, and carefully cut a few stitches before using forceps to extract the find.

This proved the most touching treasure of the tip: a tattered photograph of a baby, inscribed 'With love Vera', folded around an 1884 gold sovereign.

His enquiries led to Gareth Morgan, president of the Australian Society of World War 1 Aero Historians (www.ww1aero.org.au), who realised the potential historical value of the items, and contacted Terence Hetherington, manager and senior curator of the Fleet Air Arm Museum at Nowra on the New South Wales south coast.

The farmer proved to have rescued a trove of Little relics, improbably surviving for almost a century, just as they seemed about to vanish forever. On condition of anonymity, he donated the memorabilia to the Naval Heritage Collection as a stunning addition to the Museum's existing Little display.

Terry is now examining the finds in great detail. His interim summary of the finds, pending more research and analysis:

- Flying helmet with hand printed name 'R.A.Little' on the inner lining, plus the Latin words 'Deo patria litteria' (motto of Scotch College, Little's old school in Melbourne) and Little's family address,'Windsor, Victoria, Australia'.
- The faded baby photograph is presumably Little's son Alec, born March 1917. His nickname 'Blymp' was painted prominently below the cockpit of Little's Sopwith Triplane in 1917. The handwritten inscription is from Little's English wife, Vera.
- A silk shirt with faint writing, possibly 'RNAS Service'
- Waistcoat with Australian manufacturer's label (Keith Courtney, Melbourne). In a crease in the inner fabric, the printed name 'R.A. Little' and the family address.
- Paisley cravat made in the UK, and a black tie.
- Metal spectacles case containing flying goggles with red lens—and pressed wattle and pansy flowers. Little was known to grow flowers near his tent at French airfields.
- Two 'long johns' sets of underwear, one with the label 'Mark Foy, Sydney' (a large department store) and the embroidered tag 'AL'.
- An embroidered silk 'Happy Birthday' handkerchief attached to a French postcard with the message: 'To my dear wife wishing you many happy returns and good luck'.
- A 1898 British penny, with a hole drilled in it, presumably for a cord. It bears an obvious impact mark, with small blobs which could be bullet fragments.
- Brown leather Gladstone bag inscribed on outside with initials 'W.E.H'

- A paper packet containing four glass photographic negative plates and a handwritten note 'Please return to the Little family Punt Rd Windsor Victoria Australia'.
- A plain black cotton necktie and a brown woollen scarf.
- Medallions ('Honour to the AIF' and 'For King and Country') issued by the Victorian Education Board in his home State.

How did the bag get to the tip so far from Little's home state? As this book went to press, no leads had surfaced, despite media publicity. Research is continuing.

Contact: Terry Hetherington, Fleet Air Arm Museum, Nowra, NSW, Australia.
4 August, 2013. Email terence.hetherington@defence.gov.au. Phone 61-2-4424 2192.

Bibliography and sources

Books

Bromet, G., *Naval Eight*, Naval and Military Press, 2004

Collishaw, R., *Air Command: A Fighter Pilot's Story*, William Kimber, London, 1973

Crundall, E. D., *Fighter Pilot on the Western Front*, William Kimber, London, 1975

Cutlack, F. M., Volume VIII, *Official History of Australia in the War of 1914–1918*

Franks, N., *Sopwith Triplane Aces of World War 1*, Osprey Publishing, 2004

Hadingham, E., *The Fighting Triplanes*, Hamish Hamilton, 1968

Isaacs, K., *Military Aircraft of Australia 1909–1918*, Australian War Memorial, 1971

McCudden, J., *Flying Fury*, Greenhill Books, 2000

Mitchell, J., *The Deepening Roar*, Allen & Unwin, 2001

Newton, D., *Australian Air Aces*, AerospAce Publications, 1996

Rochford, L., *I Chose The Sky*, William Kimber, London, 1977

Magazines and newspapers

St Cyrien, K. C. D., 'The Saga of Sopwith Pup N5182', *Sport Aviation*, May 1975

Others as cited in text

Websites

Australian Defence Force Academy, www.lib.adfa.edu.au

Australian Dictionary of Biography Online, www.adb.online.anu.ed.au

Australian War Memorial, www.awm.gov.au

Commonwealth War Graves Commission, UK, www.cwgc.org

Unpublished sources

Personal communications:

Little descendants, 2008–09

Prue Minifie, 2008

Miscellaneous

Australian Defence Force Academy Library, Special Collections (MS182, Guide to the papers of Robert Alexander Little)

Scotch College archives, Melbourne

Public Records Office, Victoria: shipping lists

Fleet Air Arm Museum, Royal Australian Navy (Little file)

National Archives, UK

RAF Museum, Hendon, background on Sopwith Pup N5182, RNAS

Index